DOWN HOME MISSOURI

Dalton Elev.

DOWN HOME MISSOURI

When Girls Were Scary
and Basketball Was King

JOEL M. VANCE

UNIVERSITY OF MISSOURI PRESS
COLUMBIA AND LONDON

Copyright © 2000 by Joel M. Vance
University of Missouri Press, Columbia, Missouri 65201
Printed and bound in the United States of America
5 4 3 2 1   04 03 02 01 00

Library of Congress Cataloging-in-Publication Data

Vance, Joel M., 1934–
Down home Missouri : when girls were scary and basketball
was king / Joel M. Vance.
        p. cm.
ISBN 0-8262-1307-3 (alk. paper)
    1. Vance, Joel M., 1934– —Childhood and youth.
2. Country life—Missouri—Dalton Region. 3. Authors,
American—20th century—Biography. 4. Missouri—
Social life and customs. 5. Dalton (Mo.)—Biography.
I. Title.
CT275.V216 A3   2000
977.8'25—dc21
[B]   00-061539

⊗ This paper meets the requirements of the
American National Standard for Permanence of Paper
for Printed Library Materials, Z39.48, 1984.

Text design: Elizabeth K. Young
Jacket design: Vickie Kersey DuBois
Typesetter: The Composing Room of Michigan, Inc.
Printer and binder: Edwards Brothers, Inc.
Typefaces: Minion, Freestyle Script, Artisté

Photos courtesy the author, Dalton Historical Society, and Keytesville High School.

Frontispiece: Aerial view of Dalton

Contents

DOWN HOME MISSOURI

1

Me and Al Capone

Al Capone once lived up the street from our apartment on Prairie Avenue on the South Side of Chicago, but he had moved on to more permanent residence in prison by the time we moved there.

The closest anyone in our family came to the gangsters of the Roaring Twenties was when a bullet snapped through the window of my Uncle Sam's Chicago apartment and buried itself in the wall above his head. It wasn't aimed at him—it was just a stray shot from the frequent mob gunfire—but it made him wonder if perhaps the move he and my father had made from a hard rock farm in Chariton County, Missouri, was the right choice.

It seemed as if no matter where they went they couldn't escape tenuous connection with gangsters: My Missouri grandfather and grandmother were married by a preacher named Younger, kin to the infamous Cole, Bob, and Jim. And we finally settled in Dalton, Missouri, named for a kin of the infamous Dalton Gang. And a dead Dust Bowl hobo who claimed he had been a Capone mobster may have been my mother's older brother.

The farm where my grandparents and their four children lived was gullied, abused by too much poorly done agriculture on land not suited for it.

All three boys opted to leave the farm, though their only sister stayed down home the rest of her life. Both Uncle Sam and my father were smart enough to see there was little future raising tobacco on land already exhausted by it, and they decided Chicago, that toddlin' town, was where wide-eyed kids who'd scarcely known a new pair of shoes in nearly two decades should migrate to.

My father managed to graduate from high school (fifteen of the forty-seven freshmen in his class did not) and go on to business school before he went to Chicago and met my mother. In 1930 he gave her a diamond ring that cost eighty-five dollars. That was a dollar less than the total cost to deliver me at Woodlawn Hospital (including ten days there) four years later.

I was born at the tail end of the hottest summer on record. My mother was in the final stages of her pregnancy with no air conditioning, nothing but the humid night breeze to cool. People slept on fire-escape landings swaddled in wet sheets, anything to escape the unrelenting heat.

On the back of the payment receipt for my delivery, my father wrote rough draft telegrams to relatives: "Joel Martin arrived this morning, seven and a quarter pounds. Ann and baby fine." A second draft, probably for some of his fishing buddies, read: "Another fisherman arrived this morning, Joel Martin. Ann and baby fine." My father named me Joel, probably to end a seemingly endless succession of Joseph Vances dating back more than a century. The Martin was for him, Martin Benton Vance.

My mother was the baby girl of a rowdy family. She came, tremulously, from Birchwood, Wisconsin, a northwoods resort town barely out of pioneer days, into 1920s Chicago, where every other person was doing something illegal (including shooting into the apartment of her brother-in-law-to-be).

My mother was a sweet, petite woman, unassertive and bordering at times on ineffectual. She never once raised a hand to me, though God knows I asked for it often enough. She once washed my mouth out with soap for calling someone a "son of a bee." I didn't use the word *bitch* and actually wasn't thinking of the phrase *son of a bitch*. I suppose I'd heard someone else use the euphemistic form and so I did, too. But she heard me and marched me squalling into the house and stuck a bar of soap in my mouth. "Don't you ever swear again!" she exclaimed, near tears. I spit the soap out, bawling that I didn't swear, and that only made it worse—now she thought I was lying, even though I wasn't.

When my father came home, she told him that not only had I cussed, but then I'd lied about it. He lectured me and threatened me with a whipping, but there was no anger, no real indignation. He mostly was upset that I had rocked the boat.

My mother was the baby of a family of eleven children. Her parents came overland from Ohio to northern Wisconsin in a covered wagon, and my grandmother opened a small restaurant for the logging crews that were busy ripping the virgin forest cover off the lake states.

It was a pioneer family, with woodstove heat, coal-oil lanterns for light, and a hand-to-mouth existence. One brother lost a leg in a logging accident, and my Aunt Vic watched as the local sawbones (in the very literal sense) cut off his leg on the family's kitchen table. She was fascinated, rather than repulsed, and became a registered nurse.

Save for my mother, the family was large and unruly. By the time I was born, two of her other brothers owned Hud & Bud's Tavern, Birchwood's watering hole.

A third brother, Myron, vanished in 1936, the pit of the Depression. My father hired a private detective to find him, and the detective traced a man thought to be my uncle to Mount Shasta, California, where he had fallen from a train and been killed. The Mount Shasta coroner wrote my father, "This man was arrested in Mount Shasta on May 8, 1936. Said he was a member of Capone Gang seven years ago." The physical description was off, but he had used the alias "M. Soper."

No one ever knew for sure if it was Myron or just another Dust Bowl emigrant who failed to find California's sweet promise. The country was full of tramps looking for handouts and relief from the Depression.

My father did find *his* sweet promise . . . my mother. My mother loved my father so deeply that it brings a lump to my throat to unfold an old valentine and read:

> As to valentines—it's best
> That people's tastes are varied,
> Or, All the women in the world
> Would want the man I married!

"Don't you think so!" she wrote below the sappy poem. They were painfully devoted for thirty-five years, until she died of a stroke in 1965. My father died two years later of a broken heart, never mind what the death certificate said.

My mother and father should have been a childless couple, but instead they had me, planned or unplanned. Once I heard my mother tell a relative, "I had a cyst down there and maybe that's why we never had any more children." I didn't know exactly where "down there" was, but I could guess, and it embarrassed me to hear something so intimate from my mother. We were not frank with each other about intimate matters—what I learned, I learned from other kids and most of it was wrong.

My folks were not straitlaced—my father didn't go to church, though my mother did and even taught Sunday school. They both smoked and were social drinkers. But they never swore, nor did I ever hear anything remotely bawdy from either of them. And they never talked to me about sex or scandal.

They were white-bread Methodist/Presbyterians, secure in the middle class, so quintessentially middle America that their world was circumscribed by the country club, the bowling alley, work, and home.

My father was a perfume oils salesman, the most arcane profession I've ever encountered. He was about five feet, ten inch-

My father was a perfume oils salesman, among the most arcane professions possible . . . but I remember a rare time when we shared a boat together and he was my father, the fisherman.

es tall, balding, and with a small mustache. He was not athletic as a grown man, though he had played basketball and run track in high school. He looked and seemed soft, with not quite a double chin. He was not assertive and would be overlooked in any group of early-middle-aged professional men.

There was nothing about him particularly memorable or striking. He was not self-effacing, just bland . . . but he quit his career at its peak in favor of a very shaky future in Missouri with a wife and young son, and he got involved in several business ventures that required both faith and conviction, so he can't have been without backbone.

I sometimes wondered what he would do if a great hulking crook, some guy with a wicked knife and maybe an eye patch, threatened me in front of him. But none ever did, so I never found out.

It was only after we moved to Missouri that he hardened, became sun-bronzed and lean, more like the kid who had left the farm so many years before. Life selling perfume oils had softened him, physically and perhaps as a human being.

My father bought me a baseball glove for my seventh birthday. I had indicated a desire for a baseball glove, thinking of a five-fingered fielder's glove like that worn by my hero, Luke Appling, the Chicago White Sox shortstop. But my father got a catcher's mitt, a clunky thing as big as I was. If ever there was a kid patently unsuited to be a catcher it was me. I was pathetically skinny and had no more business behind the plate than a ballet dancer. To compound the error, he bought what he thought was a catcher's mask, but was actually a fencing mask.

So there I was in a Chicago neighborhood filled with kids who played sandlot baseball as if it were a religious rite and who would have looked at me, outfitted with a catcher's mitt and a fencing mask, the way they would have looked at a two-headed calf. But neither spectacle was likely to appear on the South Side of Chicago. I could halfway get by with a catcher's mitt because no one else had one, but I never dragged the clunky mask out, knowing the ridicule it would bring.

That was the way of my childhood: my folks would try to be parents, but either they didn't get it right or they lost interest after a while. They really needed, wanted, and were most comfortable with each other and their peers; children were a mild distraction.

My father would never have thought to get up a touch football game with the neighborhood kids or involve himself with the neighborhood kids in any activity. Instead, when we met it was on some middle ground where the activity was one he enjoyed and he thought perhaps I was adept enough in to participate. He wanted to be a father, a pal, but he didn't know how.

Fishing was an exception. We fished together off the South Shore pier in Lake Michigan, more because he loved to fish than through any desire to take me fishing. Still, I was old enough to bait my own hook and not drop the rod in the lake, and interested enough not to whine when the fish weren't biting.

We generally caught two species of fish. One was the lake perch, little cousin to the walleye and perhaps the best eating fish there is. The other, scarcely less delectable on the table, we called "lake herring." It was a slender, round fish with a blue-black back and silver underside. I can see them yet, thrashing in the water, glittering with motion. In fact, that's the way we often knew we were about to get a bite. We'd see the flash and be ready when the fish hit our minnow. They were quick, but I was quicker, a ten-year-old kid with the great hand-eye coordination that also made me the neighborhood champion at burnout baseball.

One evening my father and I were fishing with minnows off the old pier when I hooked a lake herring that weighed more than a pound. All the codgers gathered around, green with envy, saying stuff like, "Geez, kid, helluva fish!" My dad beamed, proud of his scrawny burnout champ, and I was embarrassed and dug my toe in the crumbling old concrete and warmed myself in the wonderful glow of admiration. Actually, a "lake herring" is a cisco and, many years after my big catch, I found it described in Howard Walden's *Familiar Freshwater Fishes of America*. The cisco is a member of the whitefish family. "At all seasons, its flesh is tasty when fresh or smoked," Walden says. I still remember the delicate taste of cisco and lake perch. No better fish exists.

Walden took the wind out of my sails, though, by saying the average Great Lakes cisco weighs a pound, and they can grow to five pounds. Mine would have been barely above average.

Still, small triumphs when you're small are as good as big triumphs when you're big, and better than none. For a brief time my father and I were as close as we ever got. He didn't hug me—he never did—but I could see the pride in his eyes and the pleasure that he got from my pleasure. We grinned at each other and there was a rare moment when we were connected as friends, not as father and son.

Mostly, he would go to his office in downtown Chicago and I would go to Arthur Dixon Elementary School and our lives were tangential. Sometimes he would bring home a visitor from the French parent company and I would be charmed by and shy of people who spoke with an exotic accent. They invariably praised me as a "good-looking young man," though I wasn't. I was painfully skinny, with big ears and a mop of straight hair and big, frightened eyes, like those of a puppy that knows it is going to be whipped for something.

I was shy to the point of catatonia around girls. Maybe it had to do with the whipping I got when I was about seven, a suppressed memory that festers like a tiny thorn wound in the skin of my life. I explored the differences in the sexes with a neigh-

I was painfully skinny, with big ears and a mop of straight hair and big, frightened eyes, like those of a puppy that knows it is going to be whipped for something.

bor girl by baring my butt to her. She reciprocated by showing me her scrawny rump. Neither of us was impressed. As a sexual adventure it lacked something (actually, it lacked *everything*).

Our intent was not sexual, anyway. We had heard through the kid grapevine that boys and girls were built differently and, each being only children, had no siblings to spy on. I can't speak for hers, but my parents, at least, were obsessively modest.

I knew in theory (the kid grapevine) that women were different but had no idea how. Our dog, Chaps, was female, but I never made the anatomical connection between canine and human.

After the little girl showed me her butt, which was just like mine in back, we rose from our squats behind a spirea bush, hiked up our britches, and threw overripe tomatoes at a baby buggy, pushed by an immediately hysterical new mother. I don't know why we threw the tomatoes, except that we had them (perhaps rejects from the neighborhood Victory Gardens that had been planted to help the war effort) and the buggy was what our Fighting Forces called a "target of opportunity."

My father also saw my scrawny butt that evening, only he did more than look at it. He whipped it until it was red and stinging. My father was a mild man who never swore (at least in front of me) and who never showed anger or frustration, except in those rare moments when I pushed him beyond his extended limits. After he heard the tomato story, he glared at me and said, "I'm going to cut a switch."

He left the house with a paring knife and I sat numb with terror, because this punishment was beyond anything he'd ever done. The switch was new growth off a neighbor's shade tree and after he pared the leaves and twigs, it left a whiplet that he proceeded to lay across my narrow buttcheeks.

I howled as if he were disemboweling me, and he quit after a few strokes, no doubt ashamed and maybe a little frightened at the emotional storm he'd created. He didn't like confrontation, nor tantrums.

All through the fourth grade I mooned over Judy Green as she hunkered, oblivious, over the intricacies of long division, one row over and three seats up.

This was at Arthur Dixon School, and we endured the fourth grade together, Ms. Green and I, though she won't remember me. She was a deliciously rounded honey blonde with blue eyes and a smile that could melt a hockey rink. If I ever talked to her at all, it probably was the low moan of a dog hearing a distant siren.

Skinny, big ears, the frightened look of a rabbit caught in a headlight. That pretty well sums it up. My father said I looked like either Clark Gable, who had prominent ears . . . or a taxicab coming down the street with both doors open. I'm not sure how he came up with that simile, but even then I wished he hadn't.

Today Judy Green would be in her sixties, long since married, children grown and gone, grandchildren clambering over her. She never knew how desperately I loved her, in common with other girls whom I was too shy to court.

I found other loves, but still remember that first desperate crush. And I remember my first attempt at the art of serenade. I sang "Sentimental Journey" to Helen Lipske, who lived in the apartment adjoining ours. The third floor apartments had front bay windows that were separated by an entryway.

After it got dark (so I could be cloaked by the anonymity of night), I would croon, much in the manner of Mr. Bing Crosby (had he been afflicted with a career-ending disease that made him sound like a Munchkin), and I would imagine that

Helen Lipske was collapsing in a quivering heap of helpless love just across the passageway. What she was collapsing in, I found out later from a neighborhood kid, was helpless laughter.

My father would enthuse about perfumes and my mother would listen, though I was bored silly. Perfume oils, unlike the finished product, could drop a buzzard from the sky. Beaver castoreum, the musk from the animal's sex glands, is a scent fixative, a staple in the perfumer's bag of olfactory tricks. It stabilizes the delicate fragrances that make perfume what it is. But place a dab of beaver castoreum behind your ear and you could walk through any dark alley in perfect safety. No one, at least downwind, would want to get within Saturday night special range.

Yet my parents liked to read (although most of their books were mysteries) and they were intelligent and talked about the world while I watched and listened, as if involved as a spectator in a verbal tennis match.

As soon as I learned to read I read voraciously. Books contained worlds that I couldn't imagine, but that the writers could. I read books far beyond my capacity to comprehend them. I spent much of my time at the local library, reading Jack London and Jim Kielgaard and learning about the noble collies of Albert Payson Terhune.

I dreamed outdoor dreams. I wanted to be a hunter or trapper or mountain man. I wanted to fish for something bigger than a lake herring. Maybe another fisherman *had* arrived in the world. I lived for summers in Birchwood or down home on the Missouri farm because I could be outdoors from the time I got up until long after dark and no one worried whether I'd been hit by a streetcar.

My memories are an untidy jumble before the quiet Sunday in December 1941, when my father and I were en route home after picking up the hefty *Chicago Tribune*. The car radio announced the end of what we had known and the beginning of confusion, war, anxiety, and disruption. Franklin Delano Roosevelt, the president of the United States, told us that we were at war: "Yesterday, December 7, 1941, a date which will live in infamy, the United States of America was suddenly and deliberately attacked by naval and air forces of the Empire of Japan.

"No matter how long it may take us to overcome this premeditated invasion, the American people in their righteous might will win through to absolute victory," Mr. Roosevelt declared.

I was seven years old and Pearl Harbor changed everything. Cousins became Marines and sailors and soldiers. My balding forty-year-old father was worried about the draft, though with his age and family status he wouldn't be in the first wave.

Still, there was national anxiety, almost hysteria. If the Yellow Horde invaded us, as was deemed possible, every able-bodied man was vulnerable, regardless of his age or family responsibility, and that meant my dad.

All of a sudden he was not my father the salesman, who bought me a fencing mask for a catcher's mask; he was draft material and, as young as I was, I knew that could mean terrible things. He worried about it, I'm sure, he and the other middle-aged men on Prairie Avenue. They planted Victory Gardens and practiced their air-raid warden duties. I tried to be an Air Cadet, in a program sponsored by the *Chicago Tribune,* but learning to fly looked tougher than anything I wanted to do, so I built model airplanes and played war with the neighborhood kids while our cousins and siblings did the actual fighting.

One soft summer evening when I was nine years old, with my big, stupid catcher's mitt, I was playing catch with Bob Zahorik, my best friend. Finally, when it was dark enough that the ball was hard to see, we walked through the weedy lot toward our apartments across the street. There were no streetlights. Chicagoans were afraid of air raids, as if a flight of Junkers JU-87s could penetrate to the heart of America and drop bombs on Yates Avenue, where we had moved just that year.

But there were no air raids, no war on Chicago's South Side. Just the quiet evening and a good friend. We talked about the delights of a frozen Milky Way candy bar, which was like eating a sweetened bar of iron until it began to thaw.

A trash fire smoldered amid the heat-tattered weeds at the edge of the vacant lot and something bright caught my eye. The fire was almost dead, just a few embers and wisps of smoke. There were fragments of what had been burned, charred bits of something. Scorched but still recognizable was the triangular shoulder patch of an armored division. I collected unit patches and knew that one. Chances are I had a cousin in one of those tanks.

I poked through the ashes, puzzled, and found a rifleman's sharpshooter badge—not bad, but not expert. I'd shot my father's .22 caliber rifle down home in Missouri and had killed empty pop bottles. I would have qualified expert, no doubt in my mind.

The rifleman's badge was fire-blackened. Near it was a fragment of a familiar emblem, the blue star flag. If you had a son in the armed forces, you displayed a flag with a blue star on it. If that son were killed in action, you got a flag with a gold star. A consolation prize . . .

"Why'd someone burn this neat stuff?" said Bob.

With a cold certainty I knew why. I knew that the owner of the patch and the badge wouldn't need them anymore. And I knew that someone back home, in sorrow or anger, had burned the blue star flag because it, too, was no longer needed.

I dropped the stick I'd used to poke the debris. "Let's leave this stuff alone," I said. The faint stink of the smoldering artifacts stuck in my nose like death. War, it came to me at nine years old, was not John Wayne on the screen, bigger than life. It was sad ashes in an empty lot, just a dirty pile of bits and pieces.

The war years for us were a mixture of aberrant and normal conditions. We had rationing, but that merely slowed life to an almost rural pace. The neighborhood had many empty lots, grown up in weeds, or planted to Victory Gardens, and women who'd never worried about much more than a hairdresser's appointment learned to can vegetables.

There were neighborhood picnics where everyone would gather and drink lemonade and eat hot dogs and discuss the war. We played incessant games of hide-and-seek or kick-the-can, screaming and annoying the adults.

Once, a teenage girl, wearing a peasant blouse, bent over to pick something up in front of me and I could see her breasts, an absolutely magic moment that stopped me in my tracks, mouth open. Then she straightened up and someone tagged me and I was It and the moment was gone.

Had I been given a choice of a place to live, I'd have picked Birchwood, my mother's hometown. There were lakes and cool breezes and cousins my age. The fishing was good, and the air smelled of conifers and road tar and fish residue.

My uncles, Hud and Bud Soper, owned the tavern. Once my cousins and I swiped a couple of warm beers from the storeroom and hid in the odoriferous outhouse to drink them. The beer tasted as bad as the outhouse smelled, but it was forbidden, therefore attractive. We smoked cigarettes without inhaling, usually butts filched from an aunt or uncle's ashtray.

My cousin Pat once jokingly picked up a firecracker that had fizzled and stuck it in his mouth like a cigarette. It went off, horribly blistering his mouth and making my ears ring for a

couple of days. But even with the occasional pyrotechnic set-
back, life in Birchwood was preferable to the South Side of
Chicago and surely better than the hillbilly life down home in
Missouri.

Down home on Uncle Finney and Aunt Sis's farm, the water was muddy, and no one in the family owned a bar or even
went to one. There were almost no kids my age, and the only
ones lived on neighboring farms, a good hike away.

Everyone worked from can't see to can't see and had no time
for fun. The north country had the feel and smell of Jack London; "down home" merely smelled like old cows and hard work.

So, naturally, just after the war ended, we moved to Chariton County, Missouri.

It was 1947, the lull between World War II and Korea. The
economy couldn't grow fast enough to satisfy those who wanted to spend the savings of the austere war years. The country
was giddy with postwar prosperity.

My father was offered a promotion to the New York office.
It was the big time for a perfume oils salesman. If Chicago of-
ten frightened a twelve-year-old kid, New York City was the
Wolf Man in a business suit.

"I don't wanna!" I shrilled, my preadolescent voice already
cracking. And my mother had not lost her rural roots and was
anxious about moving a thousand miles farther from Birchwood.

My father had a choice: bully the family into a career move
they didn't want or quit the sales job he'd had for twenty years
and move back to Missouri and try to eke out a living. He could
manage the large farm that he and two partners were buying,
though tenant farmers had run it without supervision for
years.

I don't know if it took courage to leave security for the definite insecurity of farm life, or if he just didn't want to get into

an intrafamily squabble, but he quit the perfume oils business and we moved back to Chariton County, the boyhood home of my father and the lifelong home of his father and his father before him, and so on back more than one hundred years.

Missouri was my home for the last three years of the 1940s and most of the 1950s. There was a sharp contrast between Chicago, then the nation's second-largest city, and Dalton, a town of about two hundred (the population varied up and down by a couple depending on whether the local chicken thieves were in or out of the Keytesville jail).

There were Vances in Chariton County long before there was a Chicago, long before there was a Birchwood. My urban roots were flimsy and easily broken, but I found that my Missouri roots tapped deep into history.

2

Down Home

Chariton County is named for the town of Chariton, organized in 1817 and long disappeared. The county dates to 1820 when it was created out of Howard County. The town of Chariton, near the mouth of the river of the same name, began in 1818 and within a year had five hundred people.

But where the word *Chariton* came from is a minor historical mystery. Lewis and Clark thought it was from "Theriaton," though I'm not sure what "Theriaton" referred to. Others claimed it was a corruption of Old French *charrette*, which meant "little wagon" or maybe "chariot."

Little Wagon County?

Actually, it makes far more sense to believe the name came from John Charaton, who set up his trading post near the mouth of what came to be known as the Chariton River (which rises in Iowa and once meandered more than three hundred miles south to its junction with the Missouri River).

An old history claims that Missouri's "climate is mild, salubrious and healthful. No sandstorms sweep over her prairies, no simooms devast her fields, nor do 'northers' scatter disease in her train." Well, that's pretty true, but I'd give a lot to see a real simoom . . . and anyone who has spent July in Missouri would not describe it as "salubrious."

I was born in Chicago in 1934 and since Chicago is north of Missouri, we called my father's home "down home." It wasn't much, but it sure wasn't Chicago. It was 160 acres of gullied Chariton County hills, worn-out soil and people nearly so.

The women were ample almost without exception, the men spare and grizzled. I first remember down home as a place with soft coal-oil lamps where twilight meant bedtime.

A little later, the Rural Electrification Administration snaked power lines over the hills and my Uncle Finney could follow the progress of his son, Roy Joe, across Europe. Had it not been for the war, Roy Joe likely would have stayed on the farm, first to help his dad, then to take over. Instead, he joined the paratroops, broke his back on landing in Normandy, and

Grandma Vance has her hand on the butter churn as if she might need it for self-defense, but Grandpa Vance is relaxed; my dad, the "least un," stands beside his taller, older brother Bill. It was a tough life down home.

fought for several days behind German lines because he really didn't have much choice.

Chariton County bred tough farm kids. My Uncle Sam once accidentally shot his brother, my father, in the lip with a .22 caliber short. My father hid his face from his mother for days until the wound healed enough that he could pass it off as a typical minor farm accident.

Chariton County bred tough farm kids.

Singer John Denver thanked God he was a country boy, his voice brimming with bucolic effervescence.—But I thank God that I wasn't. There wasn't much to look forward to when you were a boy in the country, not in my boyhood, which was in the 1940s and early 1950s. I doubt it's gotten much better. Denver's idea of "country" was standing atop a mountain with a crisp breeze ruffling his hair while he fondled a guitar.

My idea of country, based on what I've seen of it through nearly six decades, is shit—lots of it in various forms, all messy. There isn't much romance associated with country life despite the idyllic pages of the various yuppie magazines with *country* in their title. Those magazines celebrate the life of rich people living in the country, or at least people who make a living elsewhere but choose to live on rural land.

They don't deal with scours and botflies and the bawling, shuddering death of a sick cow. They deal in the rich aroma of Folger's, starting another day for people who wouldn't know a callus if it bit them on the ass. They are country people in the same sense that a dog is an attack dog if it barks at strangers.

Being a real country boy is a handicap. It's a long way between girls, movie houses, baseball diamonds, and friends. But it's only a short distance to the machinery shed, where there's a tractor you're encouraged to ride for endless hours, or to a hayfield full of bales and god-awful summer heat, or to other places that are not comfortable.

Practical education is encouraged on most farms, not appreciation of the arts. You learn to disengage recalcitrant lug nuts, sometimes even without barking your knuckles. You can worm pigs and castrate sheep. You learn to plow by headlight and get up at 4 A.M. for chores (the same ones you put to bed a few hours earlier). You learn that vacations are for people in movies—unless you want to take your livestock to the beach with you; someone has to be on hand to tend to them. A night out might be a trip to the Burger King in town and you fret over the high cost of restaurant food and realize it isn't nearly as good as what you would have had at home.

You have never, since the age of about three, had clean fingernails. You're lucky if you don't reek, however faintly, of manure and sweat. You always owe so much money at the bank that it frightens you if you think about it, but you try not to. You are God fearing in the truest sense, because God is a frightening force that sends hail and drought and flood and plant disease.

I think I worked it just right. I was born in Chicago and lived there until I was in the eighth grade. Then we moved to a small town barely out of the country (a walk two blocks in any direction would put you in a cornfield). But I never lived on a farm other than several summers down home with my aunt and uncle.

I lived in the city long enough to discover the Museum of Natural History and the Museum of Science and Industry, but not long enough to be brutalized or recruited by a gang of punks. There were gangs in Chicago in the late 1940s, but unlike today's street hoods crazed on crack and armed with more hardware than a Green Beret platoon, they probably wouldn't kill you. They'd take your money if you had any, try to make you wet your pants with threats, maybe swat you around a little, then let you go, crying, toward home. Good innocent fun.

But summers on the farm were an escape from bus fumes and traffic noises and the threat of being pantsed by some kid thugs.

Barns and horses, the smell of fresh manure mingled with that of fresh-stored hay, that's fresh in my mind's nose.

Old wooden barns, with their creaking timbers and somnolent sighs, were the perfect place for milking, communing with large farm animals, or making out (which usually translated to chaste kisses and relatively innocent tussles in the hay).

I've never had much use for horses. If I were going to buy a riding animal, I'd buy a mule. Mules have a modicum of common sense, are more surefooted, and generally are stronger, pound for pound, than horses. If a mule were as handsome as a horse, you'd never see another horse, except as necessary to breed more mules. Mules perhaps know they have been cheated of a love life, so they dedicate their lives to intellectual pursuits. I've never met a mule I didn't like, though I've also never met one that, as far as I could tell, liked me.

Toleration is the dominant attitude of a mule. Patient acceptance of that which he cannot change. Doesn't mean he likes it, though.

When I first went down home, the plow horse was a necessity. My Uncle Finney had two workhorses, Smokey and Star. The names were not those of workhorses; they were pleasure-names. A fictional Smokey was the hero of a Will James western book that I loved as a boy, so she quickly became my favorite. She was, to me, the cowpony of James's book. But in reality she and Star were there to work, not pleasure the idle hours of a city kid. They pulled a manure spreader or hay rake or wooden wagon for a living. The romance of the range, if there is any, was as fictional as the Will James book.

My uncle Finney had no time to ride horses for pleasure. If he rode one at all, it was to get to the back side of his gullied farm quicker than he could on foot. And he wouldn't bother with a saddle. He'd hop on Smokey and trot off like a monkey on a circus animal. Neither he nor Smokey seemed to enjoy the outing very much.

Smokey was a fairly small mare, patiently resigned to her dreary life. She was ridable if you could stay on her, but she looked for ways to dishorse you, and if she ever got loose, she would head for the barn at a pace just a fraction faster than the best speed a crying, cursing ten-year-old kid could manage.

Star was a large, frisky horse who looked as unpredictable and dangerous to me as a brontosaurus. I was afraid of her. Since I usually fell off Smokey, there was no reason to believe I wouldn't fall off Star, and it was a longer fall from her roof.

Western fiction is filled with horses standing over their fallen masters until help comes. Trigger and Champion actually would go to find help. What a crock. Those who read emotion into the impassive faces of horses have more imagination than I do. If the horse, standing over its fallen master, has any thought at all, it probably is, *Oh, shit, what do I do now!*

Aside from instances of obvious anger when a horse rolls its eyes and flattens its ears, I suspect horses think about as often as granite outcrops. I've long maintained that you can count on a horse for three things: To fart, bite you, and step on your feet. But I think I was conditioned in my attitude about horses by Smokey. Horses, bless their anachronistic hearts, are fading from the farm scene and I will not miss them.

I do miss Finney, though; he has been dead many years. He was a rowdy little banty rooster, grizzled and seamed. He and "Sis," my aunt, were my hosts in those last summers before we moved to Missouri. Roy Finnell married Lilah Mae Vance and

Uncle Finney was a rowdy little banty rooster, with his work hat cocked jauntily and his jaw ever drizzled with homegrown chaw . . . which finally killed him.

sired a litter of children. They were all girls, save for Roy Joe, the lanky son who joined the army and parachuted into Normandy on D-Day.

Sis and Finney (I never called them by any other names) followed Roy Joe's progress across Europe on a map pinned to the wall. They had no electricity, so they used coal-oil lamps (that's kerosene, for city folk). But the lamps weren't lit much in the long days of summer.

They worked from before dawn to after sunset and then they went to bed. No lamp-lighting for reading or other entertainment. Just crawl, groaning, into a lumpy old bed, then crawl, groaning, out of it a few hours later.

Uncle Finney was among the last few farmers to work exclusively with horses. Tractors were in widespread use during his lifetime, but he never had one. Within a few years he was dead, and so was his way of life.

I'm not foolish enough to be nostalgic about a way of life that was so harsh. I wouldn't recommend going without electricity or plowing with horses. The sadness is not for the loss of that bitter existence, but for the soft complacency that has taken its place.

After World War II, farmers began to turn little farms into big ones because they could. It became economically unfeasible to make a living on a few acres (or at least make a living and enjoy the increasing fruits of consumerism). Farmers needed ever-greater incomes to fuel their ever-larger tractors, their ever-larger farms, their ever-larger desires for television, new cars, and other luxuries that once were the province of city folk.

Those who couldn't adapt sold out to those who could. And farms grew like cancers—the simile is carefully chosen, since many such farms grew unchecked and ruined the body of the land, just as a cancer ruins the human body.

Today's huge corporate farm is likely to be owned by Japanese or Arabs or other foreign interests, and xenophobia thrives. It's hard not to be xenophobic when you're my age and you lived through World War II and saw older cousins go off to war as whole people and come back as broken ones. As I said a long time back, I'm ashamed of those feelings, but they exist and denying them would be hypocritical.

It's hard not to be bitter when you see the equivalent of the farm you grew up on turned into an exploitative dirt factory, wired on chemicals and skinned bare of wildlife habitat and scenery.

The fiction of the family farm is a familiar theme in advertisements for agribusiness—the young girl home from college who tours the family farm with Gramps and tells him of her love for the land and intent to take over when he goes to the great feedlot in the sky.

It's all very well for farm interests to spout patriotic slogans like, "Don't talk with your mouth full," but the truth is that Americans *do* go hungry—many of them. Some live in cities, and many live in the hills of Appalachia or on Indian reservations in the Dakotas or somewhere else.

Uncle Finney avoided today's agriculture problems by dying. Perhaps he would have obstinately stuck to his two horses and a plow, comfortably subsisting on 160 acres. But chances are he couldn't have done it for long. We'd have taxed him out of existence to pay for the excesses of everyone else, and his farm would have wound up on the steps of the courthouse being auctioned for unpaid property taxes. They have you going and coming.

I'm convinced Uncle Finney's stomach cancer was precipitated by a combination of tobacco juice and arsenic. He chewed what he grew—tobacco that had been sprayed with Paris Green, an arsenic-based pesticide. He never bothered to wash the leaves. He'd just strip off a chew and stuff it in his mouth. He was in his late sixties, I guess, when a lifetime of poison caught up with him.

Perhaps, in that way, he was the first of his breed, not the last, an early victim of pesticide poisoning. The soldiers who were sprayed with Agent Orange have taken their case to court. Cigarette manufacturers have been sued by victims of lung cancer. Who would Uncle Finney sue? And who would represent him at a price he could have afforded?

To me, old barns are a visible reminder of old-time farming. They lean tiredly into the centuries, their construction magic buried beneath caked manure, their curling boards hardened against time and termites. When they topple, one by one, they won't be replaced, at least not by peers. Butler Buildings dominate the rural landscape and, however efficient, low-cost, and durable they are, they have the architectural charm of a Taco Bell.

Old barns are an expensive anachronism, as doomed to extinction as the stegosaur. Even if an altruistic carpenter had the know-how to put together a building with pegs and square nails, where would he find boards eighteen inches wide? Where would he find beams a foot wide and deep, thirty or forty feet long? Not in today's logs. Today's trees and today's barns are puny, shrill little punks, compared to the mighty old-timers.

Many old barns are being abandoned because they don't suit today's farming. Modern machinery, designed to pull the world inside-out, is too big to fit the stalls built for horse-drawn mowers, hay rakes, single-bottom plows, and cultivators.

And there's no point in a haymow, that beloved hiding and trysting place of farm kids from five years old to marriage, when there are weatherproof superbales that can stay in the field.

Haying was a mixed adventure. It was hot and dusty and the chaff bit like chiggers, but there was the magic time when the hay wagon was loaded and you got to ride to the barn atop the stack. The fear of sliding off the steep, sloped side was delicious. The steel wagon wheels rumbled on the gravel and Smokey and Star farted and snorted with effort.

A gleaming fork dangled from a rope leading to a pulley over the haymow door. It gulped a huge bite of hay from the wagon. The farmer pulled this load up to the mow door, then across the mow on a carrier, high in the rafters, until he reached the spot he wanted to drop the hay. He tripped the fork and it released its grip and the hay fell onto the mow floor. Dust swirled in the sunbeams like ballerinas, and the kid below was pleased, as if he'd seen angels flying.

Most old barns I knew had simple gable roofs, no nonsense. They were utility buildings, not architectural monuments. It took some skill to raise a hip roofed barn, even more to put a gambrel roof on.

All barns had lightning arresters—I never knew anyone whose barn burned, but it was a constant suppressed fear. Missouri farmers also stood outside on April evenings, spitting Day's Work and watching gray-green clouds coming from the west. They were judging whether it was time to go to the root cellar. A tornado could turn a barn into a ragged shambles in seconds, and at best, would scatter pieces of the roof over half the county.

Barns were a constant in my childhood, just as they have been a constant on farms since medieval times.

Some barns in my home, Missouri, housed tobacco, and had louvered or hinged panels on the sides to admit air so the dread weed could cure. Most tobacco barns have simple gable roofs, but some have intricate styles, such as a gable with hips on either end or a gable that sticks far out on either end (called a "top hat") to shelter air vents at the gable peaks. Dairy barns have still another design, with a central walkway, so Bossie and her sewing circle can come in of an evening for milking and social interplay.

Finney always had a barn cat, waiting patiently as he milked the single Jersey milk cow he owned. Finney would aim a squirt every so often at the cat and was expert at hitting it in the mouth with a jet of cow-hot milk at five or six feet.

His barn, like many old barns, was two-level and deliberately dug into a hillside (pioneer earth-contact construction) so the animals, on the lower level, would have insulation from severe weather and so hay, stored on the second level, could be gravity-fed to them.

Old barns were havens for wildlife. Barn owls nested high in the rafters and kept the rodent population under control, with the help of a black rat snake or two and the ever-present barn cat. The hiss of a disturbed young owl and its ghostly face glimpsed in the dark recesses of the loft were enough to scare the snot out of an adventurous youngster.

Barn owls are becoming the most rare of the owls because of the decline of the habitat that gives them their name. The modern barn doesn't lend itself to owl nests. It might also be that rodenticides kill off owl food (and, possibly, the owl that eats poisoned rodents). Old English barns actually had "owl holes" to admit the winged mousers.

No American farmer I ever met would any more dream of eating a pigeon out of his barn than he would an owl, but the English encouraged pigeons by building dovecotes into their barns, and pigeons (rock doves) provided food in winter and, encouraged or not, every barn echoed with the gurgle of pigeon talk.

Barn swallows flickered, blue-black, through the shafts of sunlight, trickling in through gaps in the boards in those barns of yesterday. Mice rustled in the chaff, aware that winged death was possible at any moment.

There always was a barn covey, a family group of quail that gravitated to the barn, possibly attracted by spilled grain or perhaps because the weedy cover around the building was good. They were the farmstead pets, and while the farmer would let hunters shoot any other bird on the place, he made a point of saying, "Now, don't you shoot any of my barn covey!"

Finney's barn, like most barns of the time, was faded red. The "barn red" paint wasn't a legacy from Indians; it was a concoction of skimmed milk, lime, linseed oil, and color (and since red oxide of iron was plentiful, red predominated). Red also absorbed the sun's heat in winter, though black would have been even warmer (and hell in summer). Today, few old barns have any color left. The paint weathers off, and the gray-silver boards aren't even allowed to sink into the earth, like the bones of the dead. Instead, they become a backdrop for a yuppie's bar.

The urban rage for barn siding as paneling in rec rooms and elsewhere seems to have subsided in recent years, but weathered barn siding commanded premium prices a couple of decades ago until there was a danger that there would be more barn boards in the suburbs than there were in the country. For some reason termites rarely challenge a weathered oak board. Perhaps it's just too tough for the little chewers.

Meanwhile, the barn tools that built the old barns have disappeared into museums and sometimes antique stores. No one uses an adze, froe, framing hatchet, maul, broad ax, mortise ax, auger, or corner chisel anymore.

Most old barns, even if their basic structure is sound, have been reroofed, and nine times out of ten, the new roof is metal. So, even most of the old barns are not pristine. It's like seeing Sitting Bull or Cochise wearing an Atlanta Braves baseball cap. There's something out of time, out of synch. But then even historic barns in "original" condition might have additions or changes from several different eras.

The decline of the barn began almost exactly a century before I was born—when Cyrus McCormick invented the mechanical reaper and harvester in 1834.

One summer on Sis and Finney's farm I watched a huge old threshing machine clank on iron wheels down the gravel road and set up between the house and the barn. These machines would travel from farm to farm and all the neighbors turned out to cut and haul wheat to the machine for threshing.

Once barns had a threshing floor where grain was separated from the chaff by hand—the original "threshold" was a board placed vertically across the door to the threshing floor so the grain wouldn't blow out with the chaff.

Sis, proud of her cooking, loaded a makeshift table—a couple of oak planks laid across sawhorses—with enough food to feed twice the attendance at the threshing, and she would have thought she'd failed if it weren't all eaten.

There was lemonade and ice tea. (Not "iced tea"—don't you know anything?) There was watermelon and maybe home-made ice cream, a tedious exercise that made the kid who was turning the paddle—me—wonder if the end result was worth the effort.

If you didn't grow up on an old-time farm, you can't fully appreciate a real barn. My first girlfriend, Lennie Johnson, and I lay in the haymow on a hot summer day, looking through the open mow door at the ground far below. Mostly we just looked out the door, watching the summer go by, but sometimes we talked about what we wanted to do when we grew up. Get away from the farm, that's for sure! Wasps hung in the doorway like little helicopters and the clover and alfalfa smelled unexpressively sweet and we didn't know that this was a summer that would never come again and that I, at least, would never forget.

My Aunt Sis was too great-hearted to tell her younger brother that she'd just as soon he'd keep his scrawny kid in Chicago. So she and Finney let me stay with them for a couple of months each summer.

My world was books and daydreaming, not requisites for farm life. I was a scrawny kid with big ears. You could count my ribs and I was country-dumb. I had no muscles and no smarts. Once, when spending a summer on the Missouri farm, I brought fleas into the house from the barn where I'd been playing and was so dumb that I couldn't figure out what was making me itch.

Aunt Sis had a hissy when I went to her for relief. She was rarely, if ever, angry about anything, but she was angry with me for infesting her house with fleas. Her kids knew better.

Sis and Finney's farm was on a sweeping bend of a gravel road, a dozen miles from Salisbury, slightly closer to Keytesville, and a million miles from sophisticated society. The farmhouse was tiny, even for two people. They'd added on a small two-room apartment for "Dad," my grandfather. When I knew him, he was a spare man with a bushy mustache and bald head.

He had been a carpenter but now was a full-time retiree who did virtually nothing around the farm. He hunted and fished, and the only carpentry I saw him do was to build illegal fish traps that he sank in the Chariton River. What came from those traps and from in front of his .22 rifle was his contribution to the general good.

In the evenings he read *Bluebook, True,* and other "men's" magazines of the day—light years from today's men's magazine. They were filled with Jack London-esque stories of adventure in the north country or the steaming Amazon jungles and I devoured them avidly. He tolerated me in his apartment but showed me no more affection than if I'd been a stray cat.

We didn't talk; we each read our chosen magazine or book and it was comfortable. Conversation probably would have been strained and unsettling, given our age difference and the underlying fact that we really didn't give a damn about each other.

Summers on the farm would have been moderately enjoyable without anyone my age because I could invent adventure —only children are masters of that trick—but there were two

Grandpa Vance was spare and tall, with a bushy mustache; he tolerated me in his apartment, but with no more affection than he'd show a stray cat.

playmates: Maurice Young and Lennie Johnson. Maurice lived a half mile north; Lennie a quarter mile south.

Maurice was busy with farm chores most of the time, but we played when we could. Once I pinned him in his outhouse with a BB gun, rattling BBs off the boards as he cowered inside and howled. His mother wrestled the gun away from me and chewed me out. "You could have put his eyes out!" she exclaimed, the quintessential comment of every mother who ever has commented on the use of a BB gun.

My last summer down home was when I was twelve, a year before we quit Chicago and moved to Missouri. I got my first guitar, a Sears and Roebuck Harmony f-hole guitar, as suitable for a beginner as a chain saw is for a Cub Scout building a bluebird house.

Its action would have defied someone with the hands of a professional garroter, and Segovia would have suffered a fatal heart attack forty years before he did, had he seen it. My aunt Mary heard I was learning guitar and immediately sent me an instruction book on jazz guitar for advanced players. There were pages of b-flat diminished seventh chords when I was struggling with C, G, and F, especially F.

I put the jazz book away for later and stuck with the *Guitar for Beginners* book that Mr. Sears and Mr. Roebuck thoughtfully had provided. I worked hard at the key of C, which had none of those sharps and flats and other confusing symbols.

And I did work. Never mind feeding the chickens or slopping the hogs, I had music to learn. My fingers hurt and the strings rattled with fret buzz. No matter—I had a purpose. If I could learn a few chords, I could play love songs for Lennie in the night, just as I had sung for Helen Lipske. If I couldn't move Helen with my pure tenor, perhaps I could combine that with liquid guitar and melt Lennie's heart.

I was a frog in princess land, a troubadour trapped with the voice of a . . . well, a frog. Maybe if I could sing her into a kiss, I would turn into Roy Acuff. Lennie was my first real girl-friend—the first one that in some measure reciprocated my helpless adoration.

Judy Green hadn't known I existed; Helen Lipske thought I was a dork. But Lennie liked me. She was a healthy Nordic, as tall as I, though she was two years younger. She was easily stronger than me, hardened by farm life. She didn't have my allergies and her eyes were clear blue when mine were pink and gummy with hay fever.

We hiked the hills and found a small stream with an inch or two of water in it and waded barefoot on hot summer days. One night I finally scraped together my meager ration of courage and volunteered to play my guitar and sing for her.

We sat in her front yard on a blanket, close together, her white shorts and blouse shining in the dark like the moon. I sang "Sippin' Cider through a Straw," a song I'd learned from an old WSM Grand Ol' Opry songbook, along with several others. It was acceptable as a love ballad:

> The prettiest girl I ever saw
> Was sippin' cider through a straw.

I looked at her when I sang that, implying and intending that she was the girl being described.

Having declared my love, ciderwise, I decided to move through the rest of my limited repertoire. That was "Freight Train Blues" and "The Preacher and the Bear," neither of which was exactly Barry Manilow.

I wanted to kiss Lennie. Kissing at that age was not prelude, it was culmination. I vaguely knew there were mysterious regions beyond kissing, but my sex education was so insufficient that I thought a mouth-to-mouth kiss was equivalent to making a baby.

I also figured that if the guitar ever went silent for more than a minute or so, her burly father would fill the doorway to the yard, his broad shoulders cutting off the light from inside, and demand that I cease whatever I was doing with his recumbent virginal daughter. He then would stride into the yard, fling aside the guitar as he grabbed me by my scrawny neck, and he would turn me into slop for the hogs.

This I believed with every fiber in my body. I never knew a situation that my hyperactive imagination couldn't make worse.

So, as Lennie no doubt wished I would quit caterwauling and get on with "it" (whatever "it" was), I desperately searched for songs to keep the evening alive. Finally, though, I ran through my repertoire; there was no demand for encores, so I put the guitar in the case, one eye on the door where I figured Mr. Johnson would soon appear, and I mumbled, "Well, I guess I better go home."

"Yes," she replied, disappointed. "I suppose so."

With a courage I didn't know I had, I leaned over and kissed her on the cheek (I was in love, but not yet ready to start a family). I jumped back, expecting her to swat me cross-eyed.

Instead, she smiled and licked her lips. I knew then that she hoped I would kiss her there, right on the lips, but I couldn't do it. There was too much unknown consequence. For all I knew, she would drag me into those uncharted waters beyond lip-kissing and drown me there.

Just as I was leaving, she said, "Jane is going to stay overnight next week. We'll be in the tree house."

"Maybe I'll come visit you," I said, grinning mindlessly, like a possum eating persimmons.

Any male of today older than four or five would recognize a

knee-buckling come-on like that and even I, a twelve-year-old city bumpkin, realized there was a potential for something. For one thing, her father would not be sleeping at the foot of the tree, like a guard dog.

The tree house was a slapdash assortment of leftover barn boards some fifty yards into the woods across the road from the Johnson house. I'd been there and even had hiked back to Sis and Finney's through the woods.

All I had to do was sneak out after they went to sleep (about 8 p.m.), scoot through the woods to the tree house, and softly call, "Anybody home?" It made my heart pound.

Came the fateful night and I was as jittery as a cat at the veterinarian's facing a forced worming.

"You haven't got fleas again, have you?" Sis asked.

Finally they went to bed, and soon Sis's snoring rattled the windows of the little farmhouse. They wouldn't wake until milking time for anything short of an artillery barrage. I rose from my lumpy daybed in the dining room and slipped on my jeans and sneakers. A full moon lit my way to the barn, and I had seen enough horror movies in Chicago to know that a full moon was bad news in werewolf country.

Werewolf country was anywhere a kid was in the night other than his own bed—such as a forbidding barnyard with rusty-hinged doors creaking in a moaning wind. Under normal circumstances, I would have scooted back to the house and the safety of my bed, but these were not normal circumstances.

Two girls lay waiting for me to arrive at their arboreal boudoir. Lord knows what they had planned, but the urge to find out was stronger than the urge to escape the Wolf Man. So I gulped as I slipped past the dark mouth of the haymow and climbed the fence at the back side of the barn lot.

The woods were dark ahead of me. What would they be wearing? Flannel pajamas? Too hot. Diaphanous nighties? Nothing?

My heart thudded, both with atavistic fear of creatures in the night and the equally powerful fear of love's mystery.

The moon was no help in the woods. The thick canopy shut it out entirely, and I was in thick darkness. The trail to the Tree of Life was a daytime experience; I had no idea how to find it at night.

I ran into unseen sprouts and tripped over deadfalls. I almost fell into a ten-foot ravine that shouldn't have been there and realized that I was lost. This was terrible. God, who was known to strike people dead for doing less than lusting after playmates, surely was behind this. He had moved an entire forest around so I could not find my way in it. I suspected my bones would be discovered, picked clean by vultures, in some future year, by which time Lennie and Jane would be housewives with families, asking each other at get-togethers, "Wonder whatever happened to that geek, you remember, what's-his-name?"

And I suspected that the other one would say, "Who cares?"

I began to whine under my breath, like a timid dog expecting a whipping. I couldn't run in panic, which is what I wanted to do, because I figured I'd tumble into another rock-strewn canyon. Finally I stumbled into the open and found myself at the edge of the field just below the barn. I had completed the classic maneuver of the lost, walked in a circle.

Now I had a choice: I could get my bearings and try again, skulking through the woods until I heard soft giggles, or I could give it up and go back to bed. Being ever the craven little wretch, I gave it up and slunk back to the house. I lay awake a long time in the still Missouri night, wondering what I had missed, wondering why I was such a chicken, wondering if I ever would change.

The next year we moved to Missouri and my life as a city bumpkin was over.

3

The Gun

It was the 1940s, and I still was a city kid with country roots, spending summers either in Missouri or in Wisconsin. I spent more time in Missouri before we moved back down home than my parents did. They shipped me to Aunt Sis and Uncle Finney's farm every other summer.

Chances are none of my folks' relatives wanted me dumped on them for the summer, but I went somewhere every summer. The excuse was that it would do me good, but I'm sure it did my parents much more good to be rid of me. My mother and father were free to go out to dinner without dragging me along or finding a sitter. They could do all the things married people do when there are no little pitchers with big ears around. It must have been sheer bliss.

It was down on the Missouri farm that I met Aunt Sade. I sometimes still think of the dusty little woman hobbling down the gravel road to Uncle Finney's house. She looked like a flightless crow, dressed in black, hump-shouldered, restless as the winds.

"Oh, Lord!" my Aunt Sis would exclaim. "Here comes Aunt Sade!" It was not an exclamation of delight. The appearance of Aunt Sade was akin to a plague of locusts.

Aunt Sade was in her nineties. I'm not sure she was a real aunt. But she claimed aunthood and traveled from one "relative" to another, often walking many miles when she decided to move on to the next. Country hospitality being what it is, she was never refused, nor evicted. But I suspect each family offered up a bedtime prayer that tomorrow she'd hobble out of the yard and down the road to fasten on someone else.

Aunt Sade would settle in a rocking chair like a broody hen and declaim for hours in a loud, cracked monotone (she was deaf and assumed that if she couldn't hear herself very well neither could anyone else). "I heard the guns," she would declare, and everyone would find something else to do, for they'd heard that story for decades.

The guns she'd heard (or said she did) were those firing during the Battle of Glasgow, a few miles south of my uncle's ramshackle farmhouse, and they fired during the Civil War. Aunt Sade was incredibly old and smelled of lavender. It was impossible to think of her as a vibrant little girl excitedly listening to the boom of war guns.

She perched her hands atop a battered cane and talked in an almost mechanical, harsh voice. It scarcely seemed to matter whether anyone was in the room with her or not. She was so shrunken with age that it looked as if she were imploding, sucked back by time to when the guns fired and life was exciting and dangerous. It was impossible to think of her as anything but a corpse that refused to lie down.

Aunt Sade must have known my great-grandfather, William Siebert Vance, perhaps called him Uncle Bill, and also must have known his father, Joseph, who came to Missouri from Virginia before Missouri was a state. That, for her, was a direct link with a man who had been born in 1790 when the country was a baby.

My father and his father and his father, on back to Missouri's earliest days, had lived near the forks of the Chariton River, Chariton County, Missouri. That first Missouri Joseph Vance came to Chariton County in 1820 from Virginia, grandson of another Joseph who lived in Virginia. He married a Kentucky girl on January 13, 1820, and they set up housekeeping in the southern part of the new county, Chariton, in the new state, Missouri.

Somewhere back before there were united states, the first Vance came from Scotland or Ireland. Vances have castles (meaning "piles of rubble") in both countries. Long before our Hibernian days, we were Normans, rapacious souls who came to the British Isles not as friends, but as pillagers. We were named Vaux then.

One of our Vance genealogists claims a link to the three wise men, but I think she overdosed on old tombstone inscriptions. If nothing else and despite hardrock roots, I must not be a redneck. One of the signs of being a redneck is when you can trace your bird dog's ancestry farther back than your own.

Aunt Sade isn't the only echo of the Civil War for me. Another is a .44 caliber army Colt that supposedly belonged to my great-grandfather Bill Siebert Vance. Perhaps this Colt bellowed during that October 1864 "battle" (which was little more than a brief skirmish between the Union side, where my great-grandpa's sympathies lay, and the victorious Confederates).

General Sterling Price commanded the Confederate forces in Missouri that laid siege to Glasgow at dawn and had forced a surrender by 1:30 P.M. Price's army lolled around Glasgow for three days, then headed for Kansas City. When I was in high school, that's exactly what everyone in Chariton County did when things got boring—went to Kansas City. While Keytesville, six miles from Dalton, claims General Price as its own and has a statue of him in the city park, he actually lived during the winter in Fayette, a few miles south of Dalton, and he spent the summers on a plantation called Val Verde, three miles southwest of Dalton.

A relative of Sterling Price, Russ Price, who lived in the hills above Dalton, bought my first beer when I was fifteen years old. Russ wasn't old enough to drink legally either, but he was old enough to buy beer.

Great-Grandpa Bill was married in 1863. Perhaps he bought the Colt for family protection, because rural Missouri in 1863 was about as safe as an inner-city housing project is after dark today.

Tom Ronk, a friend and expert on Colt single-action pistols, says the Vance gun was made in 1863, probably assembled in May or June. The recoil shield is notched for a shoulder stock. "It's a nice example of an 1860 Colt army revolver, all matching components, military inspectors' markings, cut for a shoulder stock, walnut grips numbered to the revolver."

He values my Colt at between $800 and $1,200. You can buy a reproduction army Colt .44 for $139 from outdoor suppliers, but it won't be an original, and it won't carry nearly a century and a half of history with it.

Missouri fought more battles in the Civil War than nearly any state (Virginia and Tennessee also claim this dubious honor), but with less effect. Most were guerrilla skirmishes that more often than not claimed innocent bystanders. There were no Cemetery Ridges, nor Gettysburgs in Missouri.

The biggest battles, at Wilson's Creek in southwest Missouri and Lexington in west-central, took place before my gun was made. By the time my great-grandfather first clutched it and curled his finger around the trigger, Missouri was a wasp's nest of minor-league brawls.

Chariton County boiled with anger. Just like the rest of the state, it had sympathizers of the North, such as my great-grandfather Bill, and of the South. Add to that a frontier mentality and you have the ingredients for frequent violent confrontation.

County histories, most written in the late 1800s, never call it a Civil War or even a War between the States. It's always "The Late Unpleasantness," a euphemism that camouflages the dreary cruelty of the war years in Missouri. There are numerous stories of innocent civilians being shot or hanged without trial, just because they happened onto a roving band of militia.

Most Chariton County civilians leaned toward the South but the county was under Union rule because the Union controlled the Missouri River, the broadest, most heavily traveled highway in the state—seize the river, own the state. Union militia were not reluctant to gun down anyone who looked as if he might be packing an army Colt and knew the words to "Dixie." It's estimated more than fifty Chariton County noncombatants were murdered by Union militia and there's no telling how many bluecoats were picked off by rebel sympathizers.

Casual murder was a daily occurrence. Roving bands of bushwhackers, guerrillas, and militia could appear anywhere, anytime. No one was safe, and common courtesy sometimes was rewarded with violence.

There are stories of farm families feeding outlaws out of country hospitality only to see the head of the household or another male member shot to death as the dessert course. Maybe Jesse James and his ilk treated their hosts graciously, as legend claims, but there were plenty like him who didn't.

Anyway, my great-grandfather bought a gun. You can't blame a man, even one apparently not inclined to war (or there'd be records of his service) for acquiring a hogleg pistol.

Great-Grandpa Bill was the younger brother of John A.

Great-Grandpa William Siebert was the stay-at-home, except for getting captured by General Price's Confederates and a fumbling trip to the California goldfields with his more adventuresome brother, John.

Vance, who did have an extensive but not prosperous Civil War career fighting for the Union. John is the most romantic of the early Vances. He and his daddy were Forty-Niners—they went to California in 1849 to prospect for gold. They panned some, but lost it in various ventures and returned to Missouri in 1851 as poor as they'd left (except perhaps in experience).

John is the only one of the bunch to have kept a diary, so what I know about my great-grandfather comes secondhand through mentions in his brother's writing.

John went back to the Pacific coast in 1852 with another brother, Henry, and looked for his fortune in the gravel of the American River. He panned some gold, then invested the money in hay. The price of hay plummeted and he lost six hundred dollars.

A year later he found more gold on the Russian River, but again he spent it all. At one point, he hiked eighty miles in a day and a half through Indian country to a friend's house and, as he said in his diary, he was "full of Gray Backs (lice) and flat broke."

John gypsied around the northwest until 1857 and decided to go home . . . the long way. He took a steamer to New York City, then a train to St. Louis and a steamboat to Glasgow. "We found all well," he wrote in his journal when he laid eyes on the south Chariton County hill country once again.

Next, John headed to the Colorado goldfields in April, 1860. Having burned out his father and one brother on gold prospecting, he picked his kid brother Bill as a traveling mate. He and Bill crossed Indian territory without event. They prospected on the headwaters of the South Platte, then on Clear Creek. "Could not make it pay, so we came back to German City, stayed a few days, then pulled out for our home in Mo," John wrote. His trips west were increasingly shorter. The lesson was sinking in.

Perhaps their fortune lay in the black soil of the Chariton River bottom. The two brothers returned to Chariton County just in time for the Civil War. "We started a crop in the spring, 1862," John wrote. "But the Rebels got so bad William and I went to Glasgow 'bout 1st of Aug." He doesn't say why Glasgow was preferable to the farm, but perhaps it was because there was safety in numbers.

Great-Uncle John was the adventurer of the family, but he didn't do all that well with it—instead of gold in California, he got lice, and instead of victory in the Civil War, he got captured . . . twice.

John started a fitful military career, which included getting captured twice. He first enlisted in the Enrolled Missouri Militia, one of seventeen different military designations in the state. By 1863 he was first sergeant of Company C of the First Provincial Regiment Militia, but he got himself captured near Rocheport on the Missouri River.

He was released on his word not to fight again, but in 1864 he organized Vance's Independent Rangers and appointed himself captain. Almost certainly Brother Bill was among the Rangers and I suspect the photos I have seen of the two of them wearing similar uniforms are from their Ranger days. William Siebert in his uniform is a pretty rough-looking guy, but almost everyone was in photos of the era because the photographers made them sit uncomfortably still for long exposures and they were intimidated by the primitive camera and they glowered as a result. Didn't mean they weren't sunny the rest of the time.

And who were the Rangers? Probably the equivalent of a Neighborhood Watch with guns. They don't appear on any military records and they certainly didn't make a historic dent with their exploits.

In fact, their only exploit was that the Confederates captured John and the whole company near Glasgow (possibly even at home and possibly during the Battle of Glasgow). The family farm was almost within walking distance of Glasgow and I'm guessing that the Confederates, having made their point and not wanting to be burdened with a bunch of Chariton County farm boys, told Vance's Rangers to forget war and go home. That effectively ended the Vance Rangers and almost surely Grandpa Bill went back to the farm in the waning days of the Unpleasantness, there to live out his life as a tiller of the soil.

Maybe my great-grandfather fired the big Colt on Independence Day and passed along that tradition to my grandfather. Bill died in 1889 at age 52, leaving behind a passel of kids and a widow; the Colt moved one generation closer to me.

The army Colt is a much heftier gun than its navy counterpart. The navy Colt was .36 caliber and so-called because it was decorated with engraved naval scenes, though my army Colt also has a navy scene engraved on the cylinder. The .36 navy Colt, developed in 1851, was the gun-of-choice of my fellow

Missourian William Hickok, who used one to kill a fellow on the town square in Springfield in 1865.

Sam Colt was firmly established as the premier manufacturer of pistols: navy, army, cavalry, and police, plus many more models. My 1860 single-action army Colt was a formidable weapon. It featured a detachable shoulder stock that turned it into a rifle that, if you were lucky, could intersect a barn up to twenty or thirty yards away.

Perhaps Aunt Sade could have told me what role my Colt pistol played in the Civil War, but I didn't know to ask her this, either. She couldn't have heard my piping kid voice and possibly wouldn't have been able to jerk herself back from the long-ago to notice me, anyway.

Aunt Sade is long gone, probably boring the socks off God, but the Colt remains, hanging in a holster as a wall decoration, not a weapon to deal with unpleasantness. I've never shot the old pistol, though I've thought about it. Stuff a paper cartridge in the cylinder, sock it home with the rammer, put a cap on the nipple, then cock and fire. A satisfying "thump!," a billow of black smoke, and a mushy recoil, like the playful push of a friend. That's what I'd expect.

I never saw my grandfather shoot the Vance Colt; I didn't own it until I was grown and had a child of my own. It is an artifact with credentials, but without presence. When I hold it, it is a curiosity, but without personal memory. By contrast, my father's Model 12 shotgun feels alive in my hands. I saw him shoot it, and now it is mine; I can feel his warm hands through the sleek walnut stock. And I similarly can cradle his .22 Winchester in the squirrel woods and relive a time with him and his dog, Chaps, as they slipped through the tall trees of the Bend, looking for supper.

Those are guns with soul . . . but not so the Vance .44. I heft it and stroke its walnut grips and try to imagine where it has been and what it has seen, but it's just a tool, a well-thought-out hammer. It is not part of me.

Remember the old campfire story "Who's Got My Golden Arm?" Perhaps someday I'll be camped in the Missouri woods, watching the campfire sparks fly to heaven, thinking of olden times, when a specter will appear in the glim of the firelight and utter in ghostly tones, "Who's got my old Colt .44?"

It will be the shade of Great-Grandpa Bill, dressed in his tattered Vance Rangers uniform, and he will glower at me the way he does from the old family tintype. If I can speak at all, I'll croak, "I do, Grandpa. It's still in the family."

And I will know my heritage.

4

Moving South

When I was thirteen, we moved to Dalton, Missouri, a fly-speck on the road map, so my father could supervise the 960-acre farm he and his two partners had bought several years before. It was a return to his roots.

My dad was a rare Chariton County farm boy, for he had escaped the eroded hills. He and his brother had lit a shuck for Chicago in the Roaring Twenties and became middle-class successful, enough that they could invest in a big farm in Missouri, a section of land in Kansas and, at one time, a share of the old home place.

Our new home in Dalton was infinitely more primitive than our South Side Chicago apartment and even more primitive than my aunt and uncle's hill-country house on the other side of the county. It was a hotel, one that hadn't entertained guests for decades. It was a nightmare the likes of which my father never had, even when he woke, heart pounding, in the middle of the night, with career yips or intimations of his mortality.

The hotel was a foundling, like a starving dog, caught in the trash can by people too kind to run it off. Years earlier my father and my uncle Sam joined with a friend, Larry Pillsbury, to buy land. I have no idea how my father and his brother met Larry, but before long they had entered into partnership to buy a 640-acre "farm" in Kansas (a section of rangeland that, when I visited it years later, was as godforsaken as a scene from *Gunsmoke*).

Apparently they had money left over, and my father and Sam bought an interest in the family farm where Sis and Finney lived, and then the three partners invested in a 960-acre farm near Bynumville, Missouri.

This was the farm that my father decided to manage, to become the laird of in true Scots-Irish tradition. Larry was a portly man who talked loudly because he was slightly deaf. He charged through life, his mind abuzz with Plans. Lord knows how my father, a cautious man, ever became entangled in business with Larry.

While my father was peddling aromatics and we still were comfortably in our Chicago apartment close to Lake Michigan and the library, Larry decided to tour the Missouri operation, see what he could stir up. He'd been gone for a few days, then my father got a phone call. Larry excitedly told Dad he, Larry, had bought a sawmill. Larry considered this good news.

My father considered it as news just short of a call from a broker explaining that something had gone wrong with the money invested in Swine Offal Recycling, Inc. No one we knew ever had operated a sawmill, nor evinced any desire to learn. But the price was cheap, which was Larry's prime prerequisite to any deal. I suspect it was cheap because the seller couldn't find any other buyers.

With the mill came a primordial Bush Hog, a gear-driven monster with a keening circular saw blade in front, about three feet in circumference, with no blade guards, no deadman switch (a feature that shuts the machine down if the operator loses control of it)—no safety features at all. It was a fearsome machine that could have been used in war. I could easily visualize it lumbering across No Man's Land, its gleaming blade howling, chopping concertina wire to shrapnel, trampling fortifications to dust as scrambling Huns fled in terror.

We used this Bush Hog for years to clear brush on the farm near Bynumville (not to operate the sawmill which, I think, my father must have given away or sold for scrap). The Bush Hog was incredibly heavy. It was like maneuvering a Clydesdale by attaching handlebars to its ass. It also had a nasty habit of whirling toward the operator every time a wheel dropped into a hole, like an enraged Brahma bull going after a would-be rodeo rider.

Because it had no deadman switch, if it got away from you, it would continue on its path of destruction until it came up against something it couldn't shred. Each time a wheel dropped into a rut it would whirl on that pivot point and head in the opposite direction.

I weighed less than a hundred pounds and the machine weighed probably four or five times that. The machine would jerk me off my feet and sling me around like a rag doll. The blade howled as it ripped through tough oak, glittering like the eyes of a killer with prey in sight. My father let me run it a couple of times until he realized that I was not the operator, but was being operated.

He took over. He weighed about 160 and was fine-boned—heavier, but still not the brute that the machine demanded. He had been soft in Chicago, with golf his only exercise. But he no longer was the perfume oils salesman with the suet of business lunches on him; he was trim and lean, and his arms were nut brown from the sun.

Now he was up against the equivalent of an NFL linebacker, only with deadly teeth. The machine flung him around, though not quite as readily as it had me. I kept my distance, in case the thing decided to attack, and watched the contest. My father's lips were tight, his forearms knotted. Sweat ran down his face, and I realized I never before had seen my father sweat. He was a different man than the one I knew in Chicago. The Death Machine, whatever its faults, had bonded us against a common enemy.

The Bush Hog finally malfunctioned and joined the rust pile of Larry's other bargains, along with a killer two-man chain saw that had been another sawmill accessory. The saw took two operators. One manned the engine, the other grabbed an unguarded handle at the foot of the saw. The engine-end operator was captain of the ship, so to speak, because no one with more than half a brain would agree to hold on to the other end without being ordered to do so.

A safety engineer would have fainted at the sight of either of these engines of destruction. This was before the dawn of corporate liability for anything. If you killed yourself with a machine, no matter how poorly designed, it was your problem, not that of the manufacturer.

My father was still dazed about the sawmill when Larry explained he also had lucked out on a property deal. Larry had bought a seventeen-room abandoned railroad hotel in Dalton, Missouri. The Wabash ran trains past the hotel just across the dusty gravel street, night and day.

Neither of Larry's partners had asked him to be on the lookout for an old hotel. That was so far beyond the realm of reason that they couldn't have imagined it. They speculated on what Larry might do unsupervised in Missouri, but they didn't say, "Larry in Missouri? He'll probably buy a goddamned hotel!" My father would have said, "Dadgummed hotel."

Perhaps the hotel was perverse serendipity, like getting a ride to the gallows in the Mercedes you've always longed for. Even though a hotel was a white elephant, it came along at the right time—my father had just been offered his promotion to New York and was wrestling with his future.

It appeared that even if he moved to New York City with a big raise, Larry would find some other rathole down which to pound the sand of my father's bank account. Better to circle the wagons and hold on. So, when Larry called to announce that we now owned a hotel, one that hadn't had a guest for decades, my father decided to abandon city life and head for Missouri before his unbridled partner bought something really useless.

"But where will we live!" my mother cried.

"Well, we have a seventeen-room hotel for starters," my father answered grimly. "We can't afford anything else. We'll have to live there."

I was entranced! Living in a hotel! I had visions of bellmen and elevator operators and other elegant minions of the luxury hotel. Instead, we got mice and squirrels and perhaps ghosts, though the strange noises that echoed through the drafty hotel probably were just the groans of old age.

So, in 1947, my father resigned from the perfume company and took over supervision of the 940-acre farm, twenty-five miles north of the hotel. He would oversee tenant farmers who had thrived for years without being overseen.

There wasn't much else he could do, aside from offer to pitch hay or scoop corn. And the boss doesn't do that sort of thing. No, he would show up at the farm each day, talk with the tenants about the operations, nod wisely and feel that he was being useful when they gently suggested a course of action. It wasn't much, but it was better than being in New York with an unhappy family and a partner whose spending gene had metastasized.

Larry returned to his bottled water business and the partnership resumed its former equilibrium.

Landed gentry generally don't drive clattering old Fords, dating to before World War II, but that's all we had after paying for hotels and sawmills.

The first sight of Dalton and the hotel was as depressing as it would be for someone in the desert to reach an oasis only to find the well is dry. We sputtered around a low hill into Dalton, well after dark, three miles down a bumpy gravel road off U.S. Highway 24, which bisected Missouri east to west. The city limit sign said, "Dalton, Pop. 76." There were more people than that on the block where we had lived in Chicago.

The hotel was near the west end of Main Street. Just across the street was a looming old grain elevator that also looked like the setting for a psychodrama. It was quiet in the middle of the night, but we didn't know that during the grain harvest its au-

During harvest, trucks lined the streets, awaiting their turn at the elevator; the noise was constant, all day, all night—with frequent trains adding to the din. We got used to it.

gurs would whine incessantly, muffled only by the thundering roar of passing trains.

The trains were the reason for the hotel. The Dalton Hotel had been a railroad hotel until the day the last drummer died, along with most of Dalton. A kid with a desire for his own room was close to heaven. I claimed two. I had a bedroom on the third floor, overlooking Dalton's Main Street, plus a large room on the second floor that probably had been the lobby. That became my den, almost in the animal sense.

My mother stayed out of it, either out of respect for my privacy or perhaps fear of what she might find in the jumble. It was a hodgepodge of old jazz records, books, magazines, newspapers, manuscripts, and indefinable junk. The room looked like the refuge of a recluse. Howard Hughes would have been right at home, except for the germs.

I wrote the Great American Novel there (or as close to it as a fourteen-year-old kid could come) and listened far into the night to distant radio stations or played 78 r.p.m. Dixieland jazz records by Louis Armstrong and his Hot Five on a cheap phonograph.

Each morning my father would climb into the old Ford and head for the farm at Bynumville. Basically, my father retired when he was forty-four years old. Whatever agricultural skills he had learned in his youth—probably plowing with a horse and forking hay onto a wagon—were totally useless in the rapidly burgeoning world of modern agriculture.

He knew nothing about farm machinery, but he was wise enough to stay out of the way of it. He did know how to garden, and that's what he did. He had small garden plots scattered all over the 940 acres, a melon patch here, a bean patch there, and he would come home with bushel baskets of fresh vegetables.

My mother canned them in Mason jars, which she stored in the back room of the basement—the first floor on the street. Because it was below ground level in the rear of the hotel, it was always cool there, almost like a root cellar. That room was long and narrow, with a concrete wall at one end. I would throw a tennis ball at the wall and pretend I was Luke Appling, the Chicago White Sox shortstop, fielding it as it skittered back to me. I drew targets on the wall and pretended to be Murray Dickson, my Cardinal pitching hero of the moment, and tried to throw strikes.

When I wasn't being a star for the Cardinals, I lounged in my den in a silk robe (which may once have belonged to my father) and read novels by Thorne Smith, the author of *Topper* and other risqué books of the 1920s, and wrote insightful prose from my vast knowledge of the human condition.

The hotel dated to 1874. It was built into a steep hill, so the second floor on the street side, fronted by a rickety veranda, was the ground floor at the rear.

In the past, the first floor had been a butcher shop and a small grocery, with gas pumps in front. But when we owned it, the retail area had deteriorated into a jumble of filling-station detritus that gathered dust and cobwebs. We never went in it, save to service the irascible coal furnace. I hustled clinkers and threw fresh coal on the grumpy fire bed many a morning, and if that is the kind of background that makes a man strong, give me weak. It was cold and miserable work and I hated it. Some of Missouri's fiercest winters came during our years in the Dalton Hotel. Icy wind seeped through a million crevices, and we were cold from November through March.

That part of the ground floor was cold and dank and smelled of mold. If there were ghosts in the old hotel, they lived in those dreary rooms with the rust and oil-crusted dirt.

The Dalton Hotel had been ramshackle for decades, and it wasn't getting any better when we bought it—but it afforded a kid as many rooms as he wanted.

We lived on the second floor and climbed a steep, narrow stairwell to the third to sleep. My bedroom window gave me a glorious view of the railroad freight station and the adjacent grain elevator. All night long freight trains would rumble past, lowing for the crossing just to the east of the hotel. Within a few days, possibly because of sleepless exhaustion, we no longer were conscious of the thundering trains. I suppose people living under the grim shadow of jets landing and taking off get used to that, too.

The hotel had no running water, nor an indoor toilet. The outhouse was uphill, which guaranteed a virulent runoff right down into the cistern, our only source of water. I suspect one sip of that lethal pool would have knotted our intestines like a hangman's noose. But we didn't drink it. Instead, we cadged clean well water from our farm tenants in five-gallon cans.

So, my father's trips to the farm were as much for drinking water as they were for business. I wonder what the tenants thought of this dude who didn't know anything about farming and who didn't even have a source of good drinking water, but who was the boss.

There were three brothers, two of whom lived with their families in houses on the farm, the other nearby: Noland, Leland, and Raymond Ross. They belonged to a fundamentalist church and were God-fearing, simple farm folk and probably didn't think much about it at all—they accepted an ineffectual boss as they accepted winter winds and summer storms and other incomprehensible acts of God. I never saw any of them upset about anything, including the time I ran into Raymond's truck and put a huge dent in the fender.

I had gone along with my father to the farm and our car and Raymond's truck were parked side by side. The two men walked across the field to look at something, and I decided it was time to practice my driving. After all I was fourteen, almost old enough to drive, and yet my father had not seen fit to plunk me behind the wheel and teach me the fundamentals.

But I knew all about driving because I'd seen him do it. It looked easy. The men were out of sight and, I hoped, out of hearing, so I turned the key and started the car, clutch in, foot on brake. Then I put it in reverse, intending to back up a few feet and then pull forward to the same spot so they wouldn't know I'd moved it.

I took my foot off the brake, put it on the accelerator and let in the clutch. The clutch had a powerful spring that pushed harder than I expected and the car leaped backward. My father had crimped the wheels, so the front end jumped sideways into Raymond's truck. There was a jarring thump and the car stalled and died.

Until that time I hadn't known the real meaning of "sick with fear," but I did then. There was no escape, other than lighting out at a dead run cross country and I knew that was no more than a temporary escape, so I stood by the car, holding on to it because my knees were weak, trying to will the big concave dent out of Raymond's truck, trying to think of some plausible story to explain what happened.

My father was upset and said, "What did you think you were doing?" which was a question with no satisfactory answer—I thought I was driving the car, but I was wrong. He followed that up with: "Why did you do such a dumb thing!" which was not a question at all. But Raymond just grinned under a bushy mustache and said, "Don't worry about it."

The ride home to the hotel was long and silent. My father's relationship with the tenants was tenuous anyway because they knew so much more about the farming operation than he did, so it didn't help when his even more hapless child damaged their property. He was so upset he forgot to fill his water jugs, and we had to ask our neighbor for enough water to last until the next trip to the farm.

Not only did the hotel lack an indoor toilet and potable water, it also had no bathing facility. I wonder what guests did for baths in the salad days of the hotel. There was one tiny room off the kitchen, completely occupied by an old bathtub. But the drain was connected to nothing, so water would have run out on the floor.

Perhaps there had been other bathing areas in the drummer

days, but I never found any sign of them. I suspect they simply went dirty (they probably were gone on the next day's train), while the staff took turns with the single tub, which must have had a drainpipe to somewhere—maybe out to the street.

We, being the modern resident staff, pumped water from the cistern, then heated it on the stove for a periodic bath. But we used a galvanized washtub instead of the regular tub. If you're nostalgic for the good ol' days, chances are you never experienced them. Bathing in a washtub involves contorting like a fetus in the womb and trying to reach parts that are unreachable.

That wasn't the only unpleasant part of living in the Dalton Hotel. While my father could cadge water off tenants and neighbors, there was no way he could solicit the constant use of someone else's toilet. We had to make do with the outhouse.

There was virtually nothing that would make the outhouse agreeable. It was unheated; winter trips are legendarily disagreeable. Summer was worse, for lime only partially defused the fetor. It must have been hell for my father, the perfume oils salesman whose nose had been his working tool.

Summer also bought a plethora of insects. Outhouses are notorious for attracting wasps, which enjoy the relative quiet of such a building. They are annoyed by disturbance and generally refuse to listen to the argument of biological imperative. To a wasp, possession is ten-tenths of the law.

I would try to be very quiet when using the outhouse, but more than once I burst through the door with my britches around my ankles and an irritated wasp circling overhead like a goshawk orbiting a terrified rabbit. Now, a wasp is relatively conciliatory for an insect that goes armed at all times. Some stinging insects—like bumblebees and yellow jackets—go around looking for a fight, but wasps usually live and let live.

Still, like all of us, they have bad days.

One of those bad days happened on the only time in my

youth when I sang in public. It was at the now-vanished Methodist Church and my mother had inveigled me into bringing my guitar and my cracked adolescent tenor to entertain the congregation. Talent was sparse in Dalton, and I suppose she told the minister what a nice voice I had—and the minister didn't realize that was just a mother talking.

I worked on Meredith Willson's "Dear Hearts and Gentle People" until I was confident. Confident, that is, until the minister announced the morning's entertainment and gestured to me.

I was on! I stood and stumbled stiffly to the front of the church, clutching my guitar like a dead turkey. I couldn't remember any of the song, and I strummed jangling chords with a palsied hand until finally the opening line came to me. I croaked into it and then, halfway through, some spit slid down my throat and my epiglottis snapped shut and I sounded somewhat like a heron trying to swallow a sizeable fish.

At that moment, a wasp tumbled off the sill of the high window behind the altar and landed on my neck. Apparently it blamed me for its awkward tumble for it immediately stung me.

I think I then invoked the help of God in chastising the insect, but the years mercifully have shrouded the rest of the morning in a haze of embarrassment and repressed memory. Perhaps a hypnotherapist could unlock the conclusion of that dreadful morning, but I don't need resolution that much.

I still play the guitar every day, but I have long since forgotten the words to that sappy song. And I'm always on the lookout for wasps.

5

Little Town Dying

North Missouri is freckled by small moribund towns, victims of a rural economy gone sour. A few people hang on and there are a few shabby businesses barely surviving.

But the town's buildings are empty, their advertising fading and rusted, and windows boarded or broken. The banks have consolidated; the mom-and-pop groceries are long since bankrupted by the Safeway in the nearest town of size. The houses are small and often run-down. Usually the remaining business is a greasy garage, decorated with rusty wheel rims, bald tires, and a litter of empty oil cans.

The sidewalks, often elevated several feet above the street, are cracked and crumbling, threatening to topple into the road. But if they did they wouldn't hit anything. Few cars are parked in harm's way and few people stumble along the uneven walkways. The buildings need paint, but there is no money for civic improvement.

A "town of size" is home to ten thousand or more. Wal-Mart doesn't build in the hamlets of three thousand. If the small town is lucky, it is the county seat, which guarantees some business and a small influx of visitors—those collecting Aid to De-

The road sign says it all—with only seventy-six residents, you want people to slow down to twenty-five miles per hour so no one gets killed. Can't afford to lose population.

pendent Children or food stamps. The local liquor store also does pretty good business.

Chain-store operations in larger towns, coupled with a persistent loss of population from the farm to the city, plus improved transportation, both on roads and with vehicles, compounded the misery of the little towns. It was simply too easy to get to where the prices are better.

Although my uncle Finney considered a drive to town— first in his horse-drawn wagon or, later, a Model T Ford—a major event, for today's farm family, it's a daily occurrence. But my aunt and uncle lived off their farm, the home place. They grew their meat, did their own butchering, and raised and canned all their vegetables. They bought staples from an itinerant peddler much of the time. A trip to town was a luxury, not a necessity.

Self-sufficiency was the necessity. Were they resurrected in today's farm climate, they'd be astonished at how little the farm family can do for itself. "Fun farmers," those urban expatriates with twenty acres, probably practice a more traditional lifestyle than the average real farmer.

"Real" farmers largely scorn canning or raising livestock for personal use. Now, the farmwife buys her meat at the IGA, even if the family raises cattle and hogs. She may can from a garden, but canning is a hobby, not a survival exercise.

Before refrigeration and chain stores, people put food up. Everything could be preserved in one way or another, from pickled peaches to snap beans and peas. There may have been canned carp in Sis's root cellar, possibly caught in one of my grandfather's fish traps, along with green tomato relish. The cellar was a cornucopia of food not bought, but raised in a garden.

But root cellars and gardens necessary to survival have declined with the small towns. Dalton has faded to a wisp, along with Ethel, Elmer, Mike, and dozens of other towns that once were commercial and social centers. Some few have reinvented themselves as living museums of small-town life, catering to urbanites with a taste for history as decoration.

Only a few towns can drum up enough tourist interest to survive. No one would go to Dalton for any aesthetic or recreational reason. It was dull and drab when it was alive; today it is shy on real historical significance, at least the kind people would pay money to experience. There were two streets, both gravel, and summers went by in a haze of dust raised by the stream of trucks lumbering to and from the elevator.

Dalton dates to 1867 and is named for William Dalton, grandfather of a Missouri governor and a state supreme court chief justice (and allegedly a relation of the infamous Dalton Gang). William Dalton was a big landowner—some two thousand acres—and he also once owned the hotel where we lived. He acquired the townsite in 1830 from James Keyte, who founded Keytesville, where I went to high school. Dalton laid the townsite out in lots and opened it for business.

Dalton lies about midway between Keytesville and Brunswick, two of the three biggest towns in Chariton County, and once was just north of Keytesville Landing, a steamboat stop on the Missouri. Timbers from a steamboat that sank in 1866 at the landing provided almost all the lumber for the Dalton Hotel.

Keytesville Landing became a bit of history when the capricious Missouri flip-flopped its channel and left the landing on an oxbow lake, a mile or more from the river channel. In 1907, George Fitch wrote about the Missouri River in the *American Magazine,* and only one who knows the Missouri intimately could have described it so deftly: "It is a perpetual dissatisfaction with its bed that is the greatest peculiarity of the Missouri. It is harder to suit in the matter of beds than a traveling man. Time after time it has gotten out of its bed in the middle of the night, with no apparent provocation, and has hunted up a new bed, all littered with forests, cornfields, brick houses, railroad ties and telegraph poles."

Yes, the Missouri is a capricious bitch of a river that loves to leap from its banks and cover the lowlands, then retreat to its channel, leaving its baggage behind.

It made one of those giddy leaps in 1879 and created the Cutoff. The river sliced across Bowling Green bend and left the lake that became the Dalton Cutoff. One old-time Dalton resident wrote, "When it cut through there was a roaring sound like an oncoming storm. People left the bottom in a hurry, a steamboat from Brunswick went down and hauled some of them out. Mrs. Charles (Grandma) Hecke who passed away in 1913 at 90 told me she heard the roaring as it cut through at midnight. She got up, hitched two oxen to a wagon, loaded her five children and drove the oxen to Brunswick."

By the time we moved to Dalton, the Cutoff was among the finest duck-hunting lakes in Missouri (or anywhere else). It was a natural stopover for migrating ducks that funneled down the Grand River and its many adjacent wetlands.

The Cutoff was my playground year round. I played hockey on it in winter, fished it in summer, and hunted ducks on it in the autumn. I picked up pecans for pocket money in the fields around the Cutoff, and it never was far, either in mind or in actuality.

Once, my best friends, Karl Miller and Foster Sadler, and I decided to play hockey on the Cutoff, in front of the Dalton Hunt Club. We fashioned some sort of net and used a beer can as a puck. We had a couple of hockey sticks, scrounged from somewhere.

I was boring in on Karl, who was the goalie, every bit as intimidating as a Hull or a Howe, when I lost it and landed chin-first on the ice. "Jesus!" Karl said, looking at the ice, which showed a red smear like that left by a roadkill.

My chin was split wide open; we made a twenty-mile drive to Salisbury to get me sewed up. I came home with ten stitches and a bloodstained jacket. More than forty years later, our youngest son, Andy, was playing hockey on our lake, lost his footing, and he, too, came home with ten stitches and a bloodstained jacket—so the old saw about history repeating itself has some validity.

Once, the Cutoff had been what passes for a resort in Missouri. No doubt on a summer day it was pleasant beneath huge old maples that fronted the lake. But the lake was muddy and couldn't have been an inviting swimming hole.

Still, north Missourians have lived with muddy water for more than a century, since the plows first turned tallgrass prairie to black earth. At one time those streams ran fairly clear, except in flood. They were protected from mud contamination by wooded banks and fields of bluestem and Indian grass, and they ran crooked through low hills toward the Missouri River. The Missouri always has been muddy, but its mud came from the Great Plains, where the drought-baked soil of shortgrass prairie was easy victim to the occasional downpours.

Chariton County, like much of north Missouri, was Sac and Iowa Indian land, and they used the Chariton River and its valley as a hunting and fishing ground as well as for transportation. Then, a settler named James Loe went upriver near present Callao (where my parents in later years lived and died) and built a mill. Supposedly, the town got its name when the new postmaster blindly poked his finger at a Peruvian map and it landed on a city of that name.

In 1825, the Chariton flooded and washed out John Charaton's self-named little town at the mouth of the river, the first settlement in what would become Chariton County, leaving a swampland that bred dysentery and virtually wiped out the settlers. The survivors moved north along the river to found Keytesville in 1840. Another great flood hit in 1844, probably worse than the 1825 disaster. Despite the periodic floods, northern Missouri rapidly was becoming agricultural. The soil was too good, enticing settlers to migrate there in increasing numbers.

There was little Indian trouble—one band of Iowas threatened a small settlement but decamped when a settler escaped and ran for reinforcements. The Indians were gone in any organized sense well before the Civil War. My grandfather often found Indian artifacts on the family farm and there were several Indian mounds on the Bynumville farm, where my father was Lord of the Manor in a dirty Ford.

There probably were Indian campsites near Dalton, but I don't remember anyone mentioning spear points, bird points, ax heads, or the other artifacts commonly found elsewhere.

The last half of the 1800s was the heyday of the Chariton River for settlers. The river still offered a bounty of fish and wildlife. Then, in 1904, a farmer named Peter Vitt mounted a campaign to straighten the river.

It's called "channelization," and it is an abomination. The theory is that if you cut across the bends and straighten the stream, floodwater will quickly leave the land, making it safe for other agricultural outrages.

Channelization simply passes your flood along to someone else. Floods roar through the narrowed channel like water through a fire hose, rather than spreading gently over the land, as they do in a natural stream. And, instead of depositing rich silt, the torrent in a channelized stream chews at the banks like an angry dog.

What had been three hundred miles of Chariton River in Chariton County alone became thirty-three miles of ugly drainage ditch. The new channel ran just east of my father's farm near Bynumville, and the old bends on our farm had become stagnant and uninviting.

My father called one five-acre patch "the Bend." It was flooded pin oak timber, and we hunted mallards there. They'd filter through the trees in the silent cold of dawn, splashing down among our pitiful few decoys (some listing because a neighbor shot them on the water, thinking they were resting ducks). And my father, in the ignorance of the times, let the Bend be drained and cleared for another five acres of soybeans. This from a man who loved to hunt ducks, but he couldn't see the rare treasure he had in his backyard.

All Chariton River water, herded into the narrow channel, has one place to go: the Missouri River, along with the combined flow of all the Missouri's other tributaries from the headwaters in Montana on down.

If the Missouri flooded in 1879 when natural wetlands, serpentine bends, and heavy vegetation combined to slow the flood down, think what would happen when engineers got to tinkering with the eon-old balance of river channel and runoff. Floodwaters lapped at Dalton's lowest end in 1951, the closest the town came to inundation, until 1993, when the entire south end of town went under water.

Now Dalton's lower half is virtually deserted. The town I knew died in 1993. The Methodist Church is gone. Most of the houses south of the railroad track are empty, destroyed as viable living quarters by the Missouri's cantankerous waters. At the turn of the twentieth century, Dalton had 330 people, about what it had when I lived there. It would have to scramble to reach one-third of that today.

I used to joke that Dalton was so small that we had to import someone to come in and be the town drunk. "Dalton," I said, "is the only town in Missouri where the 'Entering Dalton' and 'Leaving Dalton' signs are on the same post." Sometimes it got a laugh, but not from anyone who lived in Dalton. In the 1950s, Dalton was dusty or muddy, depending on the weather; the buildings were ramshackle even then. There were two grocery stores, a hardware store, an auto repair shop, the post office, and the grain elevator, the town's main business. The railroad station still operated, and occasional trains stopped to pick up or leave freight.

General Sterling Price—governor, soldier in the Mexican campaign, later a Confederate hero—had a big farm just southwest of Dalton, in the bottoms. Born in Virginia, he migrated to Missouri and ran a tobacco warehouse at Keytesville Landing for a time, before the Civil War.

Though he came down on the Confederate side when the war started, and though he captured my great-uncle and great-grandfather, he must have been a pretty good guy—for one thing, he let both of them go, and for another, a neighbor said, "He was the politest man I ever saw. He would even touch his hat to a colored man."

That was considered high praise in the days of segregation. And Dalton was segregated. The northern half of town, over the low hill that fronts the floodplain, is the surviving half of the town now. That's where the black population lived in the 1950s. The Dalton Vocational School, for blacks only, was of brick, infinitely more sophisticated than the ramshackle one-room school for white children, on our side of the hill.

I found one old yearbook from the Dalton Vocational School, and it has the poignant echo of innocence about to be shattered. It is from 1941, at the end of the school year in May. Only six months from December 7, 1941. Those eighteen seniors, some of whom no doubt would realize a nightmare instead of a dream, gave a play titled *Truth Takes a Holiday,* which, I'm sure, was infinitely meatier than *The Daffy Dills,* the terrible play we put on at Keytesville High School. The student names could have come out of our lily-white yearbook: Finnell, Miller, Hayes, and Wright. I don't know, but I suspect those familiar surnames are a legacy of slaveholding days.

The Dalton Vocational School bused in its students from a several-county area: Marceline, Salisbury, Keytesville, and other communities that lacked anything beyond the eighth grade for black youngsters. Whether we realized it or not, we had commonalities that transcended race—we rode buses interminably, we put on plays, and we were into sports.

That last year of peace before the Big War was a good one in basketball for the vocational school—the team was 17-5, averaged a whomping 21.6 points per game, and took fourth in the state tournament (the black school state tournament). They also claimed a state championship in track. Altogether a good year . . . until December.

Some of the students were in the New Farmers of America, which was the black equivalent of the Future Farmers of America. Agriculture was a big part of the Dalton Vocational School. It was one of the rare areas of commerce where a black person could compete with whites to sell products.

Ironically, perhaps, after the Dalton Vocational School was made unnecessary by the 1954 *Brown v. Board of Education* Supreme Court decision that outlawed school segregation, it closed and the land was auctioned off . . . to a black farmer who subsequently used the main building as a tobacco warehouse, hay barn, and hog house.

"Separate but equal" became a catch-phrase in the 1960s as a white rationale for segregation. We will, said the racist states, provide equal educational facilities for black students, but we won't let them go to school with white children.

The "equal" rarely was. Black schools tended to be underfunded and overcrowded. Keytesville High School was a worn old building where decades of rushing students had worn the edges of the marble steps to a gentle cove. I could get a running start and skitter down the steps, ticking each rounded front with the soles of my shoes, never coming to rest on a step, much like a downhill skier. It was a hormonally induced trick, not really designed to impress anyone, but satisfying in the way that

The Dalton Vocational School today is a ruin; only the strength of its bricks keeps it upright. It has been a tobacco warehouse and a hay and hog barn since its heyday as a pioneering black educational institution.

driving cars fast or simply running hard on the first warm day of spring is satisfying.

Black education in Dalton was groundbreaking in the state—it was the first black high school in Missouri, the creation of a group of black farmers in 1883. It was a boarding school for grades 9-12. The Dalton Vocational School, all black, dates to 1931 under that name, but it began in 1908, the brainchild of N. C. Bruce, who had visions of a Missouri version of Alabama's Tuskegee Institute. He had studied under Booker T. Washington, the founder of Tuskegee. His first school was in the lowlands south of town, but in 1909 the school went over the hill on 160 acres and became the Bartlett Agricultural College.

It might as well have been on the moon. Not once in the years I lived in Dalton did I go over the hill to look at the school. And only once did any of the students interact with me on my side of the hill—the time that we played basketball together and I crossed an invisible color line.

We heard about the school, of course—some sort of Negro college or something—but I had no curiosity about what was going on there and neither did any of my friends. It was in the community, but not of the community; at least not of my white community on the south side of the hill.

If you want to glimpse a bit of the way it was, without the violence, watch the movie *To Kill A Mockingbird,* made from Harper Lee's wonderful novel about growing up in the south. It shows the friendliness between black and white, but also the unspoken rules of behavior and the invisible lines that no one crossed.

Race as an issue didn't happen until I was in college, at the University of Missouri. Everyone accepted the ground rules in Dalton, whether they liked them or not, but the university found it had a struggle on its hands, one that took years to resolve.

The first black to apply at the University of Missouri, law student Lloyd Gaines, did so in 1936 and, after being ignored, sued for admission. Nothing happened, even though the student newspaper dared the administration to face up to "The Inevitable Mr. Gaines." The case lumbered around in the legal system for years.

By the 1950s, university students generally were supportive of integration and even voted their support—but student votes in the 1950s were the electoral equivalent of water off a duck's back. Official desegregation of the university at Columbia came in 1950, several years after St. Louis University, the University of Missouri–Kansas City, and Washington University of St. Louis all had desegregated.

The tug-of-war even wormed its way into high-level politics: Governor Lloyd Stark had approved a bill that effectively preserved segregation at the university, and when he ran against Harry Truman for the United States Senate in 1940, the black community threw its support to Mr. Truman—more out of spite for Governor Stark than because of any loyalty to the man who would be the next president.

I had less exposure to black people as a kid than anyone south of the Mason-Dixon line. I was born in Chicago and black people lived thirty-five blocks or more from me. Our Chicago neighborhood was resolutely white. But despite being segregated, Dalton's economy was integrated by necessity. Both races shopped in the two mom-and-pop groceries and the hardware store.

I detasseled seed corn, a brutal job, in a work gang that was racially mixed. We took our rest breaks gratefully and together. The blacks were far less conscious of race than I was. I didn't know what to say to them because by then it was the 1950s, and race was becoming a national issue.

One evening I plunked painfully on my guitar on the hotel veranda. An old black man, hobbled by arthritis, stopped to talk. "Lemme see that geetar," he said. I handed him my little Martin 00-17. His fingers were as stiff as the rest of him, but there was buried magic in them. Notes I didn't know were on the guitar came out, sometimes muffled, sometimes fret-buzzed, but with a liquid and moving force.

Now I wish I'd gotten that old man to teach me some of the music that he'd half-forgotten, but that would have been impossible, of course. You didn't take music or any other kind of lessons from a black man unless maybe he worked for you . . . and our family was a long way economically from being able to afford hired hands of any color.

"That sho' is one sweet little geetar!" the old man enthused,

and he hobbled off to his world and I sat on the sagging veranda of the Dalton Hotel and watched the shadow from the
looming grain elevator across the street stretch to the railroad
depot and then vanish as the sun set and everything turned to
night.

6

The Big Radio

To a teenager not old enough to drive, in a town with a population of two hundred or so, entertainment was where you found it.

Books, radio, and old black men who could play the guitar—these were the seeds planted in the fallow but relatively fertile soil of my teenage mind. I didn't know much about anything, so every experience was new.

I dribbled my basketball back and forth on the rickety hotel porch or played guitar or played my few records or . . . listened to the big Zenith Art Deco console radio that was pregnant with the world. A lonesome kid always had a friend with a Zenith in the house.

People today can't imagine how important a radio was in the 1950s, especially one that could tap far distant stations. There were no televisions, no computers, no compact disks. Radio tickled the imagination. It forced you to put faces and personalities to the voices you heard. You had no trouble imagining a herd of wild elephants pursuing Jack Armstrong through the jungle. All it took was an inventive sound effects man on one end and a kid with a hyperactive imagination on the other.

The big Zenith came with us from Chicago. It was a family event to gather around the radio and listen to Fred Allen or Jack Benny or the other shows that we wouldn't miss for anything.

We were years from owning a television set. The Sadlers had a television set, the first in Keytesville. They enjoyed hours of snowfall every day, interrupted occasionally by a dim picture or staticky sound.

We had the Zenith. It even had shortwave, so I could eavesdrop on those "ships at sea" that Walter Winchell talked to ("Good evening Mr. and Mrs. America and all the ships at sea . . ."). Blips of sound cut through the static, Mr. Morse's language conjuring visions of a grimy, gaunt-faced, red-eyed sailor rapping out a distress signal, somewhere on the stormy North Atlantic as his ship wallowed in a fierce storm.

I huddled by the speaker, fiddling with the dial to make the distress signal come clear. A giant wave bore down on the tiny freighter and the terrified operator frantically signaled for help. I breathed hard as I imagined his panic and hopelessness. I knew that the signal most likely was some guy asking for the baseball scores, but it was more fun to imagine drama on the high seas.

I knew with a certainty that whatever the story behind those distant codes, it was more interesting than Dalton. Or anywhere near Dalton. I rarely traveled farther afield than Moberly to the east, Marshall to the south, Marceline to the north, and Brunswick to the west, a small world that fit easily into two counties.

But the radio brought me people speaking German, Slavic, French—incomprehensible rattles of sound that meant something on the other side of the world. I listened to those foreign languages, hoping that understanding would come to me through osmosis, perhaps by just basking in the exotic distances. I caressed the tuning dial with the delicacy of a safecracker, feeling through that radio the immensity and complexity of the world outside Dalton.

My folks went to bed, but when there was no school the next day, I stayed up, listening to the radio, always twirling the dial to find something I hadn't heard before. I was transfixed one night when I traveled to the far right of the dial and found the Mexican "Border Blasters."

Dr. John Brinkley pioneered the powerful Mexican transmitters that covered the United States with advertisements for his miraculous goat-gland operations. Injections of pureed goat testicles were supposed to energize desperate men. I certainly had no need for goat glands. I had enough of my own—if anything, I needed to lose a few. But between the copious advertisements was music that tugged at me—the Carter Family, Roy Acuff, Bradley Kincaid, songsters of the 1930s and 1940s whom you wouldn't hear on very many American stations.

The Border Blasters had been on the air since my birth, but I didn't listen to them until we moved to Dalton. I found XERF near the top of the AM dial, in the 1500s. It was up there because, thanks to the mysterious powers of amplitude modulated radio, signals at that end of the dial traveled better than those farther down.

Dr. Brinkley advertised himself as "a member of the National Geographic Society," so how could anyone doubt his medical skills? Dr. Brinkley had been discredited and was dead (in 1942) before I discovered his station, but the outrageous hucksterism of the 1950s wasn't much removed from that of the 1930s. They were still selling things that anyone with half a brain wouldn't buy.

By the beginning of the 1950s, XERF was equipped to send you a hundred baby chicks from the Allied Hatchery, regularly $5.95 "for only four dollars and ninety-five cents per hundred. Now at this price we, of course, don't guarantee color, breed, or sex, but we do guarantee healthy day-old broiler-type chicks, which are sent to you on a 100 percent guarantee of satisfaction or your money back."

I was tempted by the baby chicks, but I was simultaneously enduring servitude in the blue-clad ranks of the Future Farmers of America. It was painfully obvious that anything connected with animal husbandry was like a crapshoot with men called Swifty and Flash, so I resisted the temptation, along with that of the phosphorescent picture of the Last Supper on vinyl and one hundred "finest quality, extra-sharp, double-edged razor blades for only one dollar." At the rate my whiskers grew then, that would have been a lifetime supply.

While my folks read the latest Erle Stanley Gardner mystery upstairs, I fiddled with the dial on the big radio, trying to make XERF come in a little clearer. I put up with endless advertisements for pictures of Jesus that glowed in the dark, and for patent medicines that would cure dread diseases—just to hear three minutes of the Carter Family singing "Keep on the Sunny Side."

The Carter Family, as whiny-voiced as they were, nevertheless spoke to me. Maybelle's distinctive guitar strum was like what I wanted to do. And their songs were wonderful, even if they did render them in a nasal hill twang that sounded like a shop saw in cured oak.

I thought that A. P., Sara, and Maybelle lived in Del Rio and went into the station at 2 A.M. to play, resting between songs while some hoarse announcer peddled miracle salves. It never occurred to me that the group was transcribed.

The 1950s saw the last gasp of live performance on radio. There were countless home-grown radio shows, usually early in the morning, to catch the farmers going to the barn, or at noon when the farmers came in for lunch. Every small-town radio station had its "Roundup Time" with a local country

band, livestock reports, weather, and commercials for imple-
ment dealers or seed corn distributors.

I listened to them avidly. Most shows had a hokey band-
leader who wasn't good enough for the Grand Ol' Opry on his
best day, but who could plug along on a few songs. There often
was a brother duo, usually mandolin and guitar, patterned on
the Bailes Brothers or Mac and Bob or the Blue Sky Boys or, for
the most ambitious, the Monroe Brothers, Bill and Charlie.

During World War II, Finney would come in from the tobacco patch at noon, put away a thumping big lunch, settle in
front of the radio for a little while to listen to the market reports and maybe a couple of songs, and then doze off for a few
minutes before heading back to the ever-patient Smokey and
Star.

I was the only one who listened to the market reports in our
house. My mother would be busy listening to the safety valve
on the pressure cooker chattering as she canned what my father was busy gathering at the farm. And I really didn't care
what canners and cutters were bringing, just what Bill and Sam
(or whoever) were singing that day. I tried to thunk along, but
by the time I figured out what key they were in, the song was
over.

Of all the network shows, *Amos 'n' Andy* was the most popular. Two white men doing blackface routines. Freeman Gos-
den and Charles Correll ("Amos" and "Andy," respectively)
portrayed every stereotype of blacks: the shiftless, two-timing
Kingfish, always scamming, always devious; Amos, who was
averse to work; and Lightning, who was stupid. Yet from 1928
through the early 1950s the show was popular with most blacks
as well as whites. There were isolated protests from black
groups that the show characterized blacks unfavorably . . . but
most black people also defended it and enjoyed it as much as I
did. I'm sure that on the back side of the hill from where I lived

the black community was listening to *Amos 'n' Andy* even as I was.

I can remember Andy's deep bass as clearly as I can remember my father's voice. Radio filled our home and the voices from the old Zenith were as familiar as those around the supper table.

Ethnic humor was everywhere on radio. Fred Allen had his drunken Irishman, Ajax Cassidy, but that was acceptable because Allen himself was Irish. We were less touchy in the 1950s in many ways. And *Amos 'n' Andy* was compassionate. We liked the characters, warts and all. We laughed at Andy's shiftlessness, but we did not ridicule him for it or think of him as "black shiftless." We knew he was good-hearted and without malice. And when he explained the Lord's Prayer to his daughter Arabella each Christmas, we puddled up with emotion.

The radio was my imagination's ticket out of Dalton. The most sought-after station on Saturday night was WSM, the home of the Grand Ol' Opry. Not by my parents, but by me. They were not much interested in music—maybe a little big band by Ben Bernie or the Dorseys, but that was about it. They wouldn't seek it out. And they certainly would not have fine-tuned distant WSM to hear the Opry.

WSM broadcast most of the day, but it didn't gather enough muscle to reach central Missouri until sundown. If I was lucky and the gods of country music were smiling, I could begin to pick it up around 6 P.M. It maintained strength until 1 A.M. when Ernest Tubb's Record Shop finished its live broadcast. That's when I signed off, though the station didn't. Someone played country music records the rest of the night, but not for me.

Those distant, nasal voices had filled my heart and head for seven hours. I remember Hank Williams's debut on the Opry in 1949, an event like none before nor since. He sang "Lovesick Blues," an old 1920s song, and the ovation went on and on. He got six encores, unheard of. Hank Williams was the quintessential flawed hero, writer of enduring songs, beloved by his fans, and prey to every vice that kills.

I tried singing like Hank Williams, which really must have set my mother's teeth on edge when I caterwauled "Lost Highway." It's not that I really liked Hank Williams's voice, but I loved his songs and bought all his records. When he sang, "I'm So Lonesome I Could Cry," I went out on the balcony, careful not to make noise that would wake my parents, and looked at the moon over the grain elevator and wondered what would become of me. After all, Saturday night was not created for teenage kids to listen to the Grand Ol' Opry. My peers were parked on secluded gravel roads with their dates, playing an ancient game.

And I was listening to the keening voice of an Alabama hillbilly and looking at the moon over a silent grain elevator.

Sometimes something happens in your youth that sticks with you through the decades of change, evolution, maturation—and nothing can change that initial impact. It happened to me when Ernest Tubb played a record by "the late, great Jimmie Rodgers." I'd never heard of Jimmie Rodgers.

Jimmie Rodgers . . . the Father of Country Music and the first inductee into the Country Music Hall of Fame. He'd been dead for more than fifteen years when I heard him that first time. It was a sultry summer night. There was a midnight train that clattered past across the street from the hotel. The locomotive wailed at the Dalton crossing and swept past the hotel to the west, as the old timbers and peeling siding of the ramshackle hotel shuddered and rattled in harmony.

Then the train was gone, and it was quiet again; I turned up the volume a bit on the Ernest Tubb Record Shop because I heard a guitar almost ghostly in its tinny, faraway sound. The song was "Away out on the Mountain," an allegorical ballad about going to a land "where the beavers paddle on walkin' canes."

Jimmie Rodgers's voice came through the big Zenith radio that I'd appropriated for my "den." His arid voice carried the ghostly whisper of Dust Bowl zephyrs, blowing across a parched land. That lean voice and his unadorned guitar sounded as lonesome as I felt. It had simple chording and single-string runs that I could do myself.

Jimmie Rodgers played a guitar not very well, and neither did I. It seemed that we had many similarities. We didn't, of course, but something in his voice spoke to the loneliness in me. I still listen to him a half-century later, singing about high-powered mamas and the mean blues you get with tuberculosis.

When I took up the guitar a few years before, it was partly because I wanted to impress girls. Now I sat alone on the sagging porch of a doddering old building in a backwater town with my guitar. There were no lights, save a dim bulb over the darkened depot building across the street. My parents had long since put down Perry Mason's latest courtroom adventure and were asleep.

I sang softly about a wonderful place where beavers paddle on walking canes—not for a girl, but for myself.

7

The Three Friends

We were an unlikely trio: a lifelong farm boy, a son of the school superintendent, and an immigrant from Chicago—Karl Miller, Foster Sadler, and me. But we bummed around for all our high school years. Karl was a year younger than Foster and me, but the age difference wasn't enough that we treated him like a young pup.

We were fellow young pups, dumb as chickens about most things, but with one attribute that most Chariton Countians lacked. We wanted to know what was going on, not just between Brunswick and Salisbury, but anywhere. We read real books, without pictures and heroes that wore capes.

We thought, however, we were far more sophisticated than we were. Others may have worshipped John Wayne on the movie screen, but my hero was David Niven, who smoked a cigarette with such languid grace that it made you want to take up smoking. And when Karl and I did start smoking, we discovered English Ovals and thought that sneaking behind the school to suck on an English Oval was pretty suave. And it was ... for Chariton County.

Foster didn't smoke. He was perpetually in training either

Karl and I were not 1950s Rebels without a Cause—we were rebels without a clue . . . but well-dressed.

for basketball or baseball. But he shared the occasional beer with us under the assumption that beer is a form of training food. We loyally began with and continued to drink (occasionally) Griesedieck Beer, because that brewery sponsored our beloved St. Louis Cardinals.

Smoking was a less critical sin than drinking, but I didn't

want my parents knowing I did it, even though both of them smoked, and I certainly did not want Mr. Sadler to know it. Not only would he suspend me from the basketball team, he would fix me with The Look and that was akin to being dealt with by Vlad the Impaler.

My father was a tolerant man who couldn't have frightened a whipped cur. He was too kind by half. But Mr. Sadler was a fearsome presence. Once, Karl—by then a major in the Marines, with combat experience—stopped to visit the Sadlers.

"I couldn't smoke in front of him," he said. "I was afraid."

The last time I saw Mr. Sadler, he was eighty-seven years old, surrounded by four of his 1952 players (three starters and me). Each of us, now over sixty, felt exactly the same way we felt at practice—intimidated. He still had The Look and he still treated us like half-assed kids, but with great affection.

Once, when Foster and I were juniors and Karl was a sophomore, we inveigled a high school senior into buying us a case of Country Club beer. "I can't get you no Greasy," he said when we specified Griesedieck. "You take what you get."

We camped over a weekend at my father's farm near Bynumville and drank all the beer. We really didn't want that much beer, but we couldn't take it home. We got bloated and full before we got drunk. It was primitive male bonding. Did we tell our dreams, share our secrets? Was this a retreat of teenage epiphany where, through sharing our thoughts, we glimpsed a future? Was there a shining moment when we transcended the crassness of teenhood and were ennobled?

Our conversation would have stunned a lab rat. "You ever try to get a mental picture of Mr. Schmid doin' it?" I asked. Foster snorted beer through his nose.

"Or takin' a dump!" Karl roared. This was Vo-Ag humor. Our Vocational Agriculture teacher despaired of ever making anything of us. He had taught generations of boys the miracles of crop rotation, but a couple of town kids and the poor farm boy they'd corrupted were beyond him.

We talked about Stan Musial, the St. Louis Cardinal superstar. He was a near-religious figure to us. Jesus might walk on water, but he couldn't hit .367. We knew that Stan the Man couldn't part the Red Sea, but we were sure he could hit a line drive over it. A close second to Stan the Man was Enos Slaughter, who epitomized hustle long before Pete Rose earned his Charlie Hustle nickname.

We thought Slaughter was everything we wanted to be, not realizing he was a virulent racist who was among the most intolerant ballplayers in the major leagues when Jackie Robinson broke the color barrier. So Slaughter wouldn't have had much use for me, anyway, because I used a bat endorsed by Larry Doby, the first black player in the American League.

Karl and Foster and I didn't even talk about the most favorite subject of a majority of teenage boys then and now: cars. Why not? Because we didn't have one among us. We all relied on the good offices of our fathers to get a car for even the most insignificant trip. That Karl had gotten use of the family car for two days was a monumental concession, made only because the family also had a pickup truck and thus could spare the car.

And we didn't talk about girls. Foster was the only one with a girlfriend and that meant we couldn't trade confessions. If he told us something intimate about his mate-of-the-moment, we didn't have anything to swap, so he didn't tell us anything. He wouldn't have anyway. There were a few kiss-and-tell guys, but not us.

We had brought our ball gloves and we played catch. Playing catch was a wordless activity that could go on for hours with virtually no conversation, except "Sorry!" when you threw a ball in the dirt or over the other guy's head. The only sound was the slap of the ball in the leather of the pocket. I worked on my knuckleball, which meant I said "Sorry!" quite a few times.

We cautioned Foster not to throw any curves and to ease up on a fastball. Just catch—lazy loopers thrown with easy motion. Just whiling away a sweet summer day in a life that would never end. Then we'd hunker down for another beer and tell each other how good it was.

We didn't talk to each other about our troubles because we weren't there to deal pain; we were there to have a good time and be comfortable. I'm not sure what those troubles were—mine were inchoate longings that Chariton County couldn't satisfy, longings for experience and understanding and maybe a girlfriend. Anybody who worships David Niven, pretends to be him while wearing a hand-me-down lounging robe while listening to Bessie Smith records in a rattletrap old hotel, has some identity problems.

Karl knew who he was—a farm boy, but one who would go to college to learn something else, with kindly parents who would encourage him in whatever he did. Karl only wished he could move with the fluid grace of Stan Musial. Karl's father had been captain of the University of Missouri's first wrestling team, and Karl had the build of a wrestler, not a center fielder.

Though we didn't know it, Foster was plagued by depression all his life. He concealed it well, but it ran in the family. An uncle had been similarly afflicted, and apparently there were others. Life would never be easy for him, even when it was. He always hid his dark days from his friends and, I think, used us as a counterbalance to his bleak moods. We didn't know he needed cheering up; he just cheered up when he was with those who were cheerful. It was only when he was alone that he darkened.

Finally we drained the last beer of that long weekend and realized we'd run out of baseball conversation. It was time to go home. "I gotta pee," Karl said and went into the bushes.

While he was gone, Foster and I jacked the back end of the 1937 Chevrolet barely off the ground. Karl returned and started the wheezing machine and clanked it into gear. The clutch was so worn that it was a miracle if he got it into any gear, and it sounded like someone dropping a bowling ball into a drainpipe. He eased out on the clutch and gave it some gas. The engine revved and nothing happened. Karl turned white as Foster and I smirked. "What's the matter, won't it go?" Foster asked. He snickered.

"Goddamn it, it's not funny!" Karl exclaimed in a high voice. He thought he had done the unthinkable—broken the family car. I knew his agony, having once thrown a rod in our Ford. Getting caught smoking or drinking was bad, but those sins were not nearly as bad as breaking the family car. Telling your father you stuck a knife in the Chevy's heart is a confession from a nightmare.

We were thirty miles from home, reeking of illicit beer . . . and Karl had ruined the old Chevy. His father was a mild-mannered man, but not a meek one. Karl no doubt had visions of being pinned by his wrestling father, possibly like an insect specimen. "My God, what am I gonna do!" he moaned. He twisted the steering wheel as if maybe that would encourage the old car to start acting right again.

We commiserated and told him it probably would work out for the better—induce his folks to get a car manufactured at least within a decade of the present. "Maybe it's something in the transmission," I said, having no idea then or now where the transmission is and how it works. "Maybe we can fix it."

"Yeah," Foster said. "Go look at it and see if you can figure out what's wrong." Karl looked narrowly at us. We were not nearly concerned enough, and it began to dawn on him that the problem might be us, not the car. He got out and circled the car, looking for broken bones. And then he noticed the jack and the spinning rear wheels.

He came back to the driver's side window and leaned in. "You sons of bitches," he said. We laughed, but somehow it wasn't as funny as we thought it would be. We had scared him and our laughter was at his expense. It wasn't the kind of joke you pull on a buddy. We had forced him into showing an emotion he didn't want to show, and he didn't laugh with us. We had embarrassed and hurt him.

The comfortable ease of our campout was gone. We rode home in a silence that was no longer companionable. I vowed never to pull another practical joke. The hurt cuts both ways.

With Foster playing Legion baseball a couple of times a week, our trio most of the time became a duo, Karl and me. We swam at Sasse's Hole, a "blue hole" adjacent to the Dalton Cutoff, possibly spring fed. It was clear-watered, in sharp contrast to the muddy old Cutoff. The Cutoff, three miles south, was a playground for Dalton kids, just as it had been a playground for Daltonites for more than a century.

Sasse's Hole had high sand banks from which to dive, and someone had built a floating platform where you could sprawl in the hot summer sun. It would have been an ideal place to bring girls, if we'd had girls to bring. Once, a classmate with a car did bring a couple of girls, and they splashed and giggled while we showed off with jackknife dives off the high sand banks.

I was cautious about diving too recklessly because the only male swimming suit in our family belonged to my father, and it fit me like a gunnysack.

When we weren't swimming at Sasse's Hole, Karl and Foster and I roamed the country together. Our world centered around the Dalton Cutoff, that muddy oxbow of the Missouri River. It was (and, in seriously altered form, is) two and a half miles southwest of Dalton.

A trickle of water runs from the Cutoff to the Missouri River a little over a mile on south. The Sasse brothers owned the land on which the clubhouse stood. Tyson Knight, who was a Will Rogers type, built the clubhouse in the 1930s.

He managed the Dalton Hardware and Lumber Company from 1925 until he died. He was a genial one-armed man who gave little kids candy bars and expounded from his throne in the hardware store. He died in 1951 and it was only slightly unsettling to know someone who died. One day he was there, the next he was not. I couldn't fix "dead" in me as a fearsome concept.

Death remained an abstract until one night when my father drove me to Glasgow to visit a doctor because I had impetigo, which left a horrific scab on my chin. (It put a definite damper on my date at the junior-senior prom.) It was after dark and we parked, waiting for the doctor to show up at his office—this was when doctors would answer a call, even at night.

We saw an ambulance deliver a body to a funeral home. It was my first real glimpse of death, and it has stuck in my mind, disquieting, like an old thorn in flesh.

Yet death still was something under a sheet that took place in the night. It did not touch me, nor those close to me. It was a specter no more fearsome than a Wolf Man film at the El Jon. And then Karl and Foster and I became friends with the caretaker at the Dalton Cutoff Hunt Club. I think the old man's name was Paul Harper, but I'm not sure, and it doesn't matter. He was just an old man when we met him, manager of the Dalton Cut-Off Hunting and Fishing Club, "The World's Best Place to Hunt, Fish, Rest, and Eat."

He was a spare gentleman with white hair, who wore a plaid shirt buttoned all the way to the collar. The old man prowled around the clubhouse in the still hours before dawn, joking with the hunters and making sure they knew where they were going on the dark lake.

He was weathered, like maybe he'd been left out too long. He wore a ball cap and worn clothing, but he was always cleanly shaven and neat. He was out of bed long before the hunters, ensuring that the cook had the coffee ready and breakfast going by the time the first grumbling, disheveled hunter rose.

The club when I knew it was a bunch of successful businessmen who liked to hunt ducks and who had discovered the Missouri River oxbow. When the Missouri River cut through the neck of a bend in 1879, it left fourteen hundred acres of muddy, shallow lake, flanked by pin oaks whose feet were always wet.

The club today is a pitiful shadow of what it was in the 1950s when redleg mallards rode the north wind down and settled in the flooded woods to the west, the hens chattering like so many callers on a radio Kitchen Klatter show.

You got out of the car in the star-shot night, no hint of light to the east across the bean fields, and you could hear the bossy hen mallards gossiping above the crowd noise of countless other ducks.

Karl and Foster and I were inseparable, full of goofy hormones and short on common sense. We picked up pecans in the fields near the Cutoff for a dime a pound and kept a shotgun handy in hopes that ducks returning to the Cutoff would fly low enough for a pass shot.

The Dalton bottoms are freckled with huge old pecan trees, and nearby Brunswick labels itself "The Pecan Capital of Missouri." No one cuts a pecan tree in Chariton County. Pecans are an annual crop, just as are corn and beans, and if a tree is in the middle of a crop field, the crop takes a detour around it.

I don't remember why we first stopped at the Cutoff and met

the old man—we were probably yearning for a chance to hunt, really hunt, the Cutoff ducks. But we had no money to rent a blind.

The old man had time after the dudes went to the blinds to spend with three kids who clattered into the clubhouse yard in Miller's old Chevy. He talked about thousands of dawns over duck marshes and how to turn ducks with a battered wood caller cupped in a weathered old hand whose fingers were gnarled by hard work and the sharp aches of arthritis.

He'd show us the hail call and the feeding chuckle, and how you talked to ducks on the inward leg of their swing with soft, contented hen noises. We weren't apt pupils, if he was thinking to train contest callers—but I doubt that he was. He could remember how it was when he was young and didn't know anything.

He would be fussing with busted-up decoys or dinking with a rusty oarlock or maybe sweeping out the hunt club when we stopped, and he'd smile and sit to talk.

The club hunters were from a world we didn't comprehend. The owner of a huge truck line had a blind rumored to sport a stove where they fixed brunch. Once, according to legend, Missouri's lieutenant governor chased the governor out of that blind after a drunken argument. Or maybe it was the attorney-general or secretary of state. Whoever they were and whatever happened, it was no part of us. We never argued, drunk or not (well, not, actually, since we never were drunk enough to argue).

One season, my father and I hunted the shoreline of the Cutoff on a friend's farm directly across from the big blind with the heater. We didn't have a heater, only a thin screen of willow shoots between us and the harsh northwest wind.

We got the leftovers, the few birds that swung a little wide of the huge spread of a hundred or more decoys, spotted our pathetic dozen papier-mâché foolers bobbing diffidently in the chop, and set their wings for a look-see.

One of the years, my father sprang for a real hunt at the club in one of the few for-rent blinds. Most of the rental blinds weren't worth the money. They were out of the flight patterns, only marginally better than our sketchy willow-branch affair. But the old man, my friend, took care of us. "Take the number-four boat," the old man told us. "That's the blind on the island. Oughta be quite a few mallards."

We rowed across the lake to the blind, sometimes breaking ice a quarter-inch thick. The decoys were locked in the ice, and my dad rowed among them to break them free. Some wore silvery girdles until the midmorning sun warmed them.

We killed a few ducks. The old man was pleased for us.

Every kid needs an old man. My dad couldn't be that old man for me because he didn't know any more about hunting ducks than I did, and he was just about as bad a shot as I was. I needed an old man to pester. I had to find an old man to teach me about waterfowl hunting, one patient with dumb questions from kids who didn't know anything.

One day Foster and Karl and I stopped at the Cutoff and the old man wasn't there. "He's sick over to the hospital in Moberly," said the cook. "It don't look too good."

"What's wrong?" I asked.

The cook shrugged. "I guess mostly he's old."

Karl and Foster and I drove thirty miles to the hospital to visit the old man, which we would not have done individually. But he had been kind and let us hang around and soak up hunting as it used to be, and we wanted to cheer him up. When people were sick, you cheered them up and they got better.

As far as I know, the old man had no relatives. He'd never talked about family, anyway. There wasn't anyone in the hospital room but him. Just him in the bed, white as parchment, whispering weakly to three teenagers with whom he'd spent a little time before he took sick.

"I'm glad you boys came," the old man said, his voice the rustle of cornstalks. He was plugged in to an oxygen system and I wondered if those silvery plastic tubes ran clear down to the heart of him.

We shuffled and murmured about coming back and how we'd see him when he got better and came back to the club.

And then we were out in the quiet hall, uneasy with the stink of disinfectant. We never saw him again. He died a few days later. He was the first friend I knew who didn't get better, the first who died.

Someone once wrote, "Old dogs shouldn't cross the road, and old men shouldn't live too long." And, all these years later, I still don't know if that old man lived too long or not long enough.

8

Tampering with Religion

Of all the sports at Keytesville High School, basketball was preeminent. Baseball season was short, a few games in the last chill of spring before the school year ended, then a few more during the summer with a pickup team, or with the distant American Legion team in Salisbury if you were good enough, which I wasn't.

There was no football at Keytesville High School. Track was a joke. We had just two hurdles for the school's premier hurdler to practice on. I became the school's premier hurdler. I was just good enough to qualify, which meant I had to run in both the preliminary heat and the finals, but I was bad enough to finish near-last in every final race of every meet.

Basketball was the glamour sport. Any dinky little school could accumulate five starters and a couple of subs and launch a basketball team. There were towns in the area with a population of two hundred that were competitive in basketball.

We had one of the best teams in Keytesville's history. We ultimately lost our bid to advance in the state tournament to another team in our conference, whose center later started for the University of Missouri. They weren't better than we were; they were just bigger.

My role on that team was puzzling, both to me and to my coach. My basketball career was much like everything else I did—sputtering and spitting like a damp wood fire. Sometimes I gave off sparks; other times I merely smoldered.

I stepped off the school bus at Keytesville High School the first day after we moved from Chicago to Dalton. I was a stranger in a strange land. I'd just endured a hour and a half on a clattering school bus, much of it before dawn, with kids I didn't know. Dalton kids were first on the bus in the morning and last off in the evening, and the bus route was thirty-five miles long.

"You play basketball?" asked a jug-eared farm boy. I guess he figured anyone from Chicago knew everything there was to know about jump shots, which were an almost-new phenomenon in 1948. Most coaches still were teaching a two-handed set shot, and anyone who jumped up in the air and pushed the ball at the basket was likely to get benched for a good ass-chewing: "What the hell kind of shot was that?"

I said, "Sure." I had played basketball.

What I meant was that I had awkwardly dribbled a basketball and shot at a rusty, sagging, and netless rim in the alley behind our Chicago apartment, in company with other neighborhood kids who didn't know anything about the game, either. Baseball had been our passion. We played baseball in Chicago until it got too cold, then we threw iced snowballs at passing cars, keeping our arms limber (not to mention our legs, when a driver took exception and chased us for several blocks).

But what the jug-eared kid meant was exactly what he said: "You play basketball?" As in: know how to play defense, dribble with either hand, shoot a variety of shots, and have a rudimentary knowledge of the game's rules.

Within seconds, he'd dragged me into the gym and I was in

a pickup game. These unsupervised spare-time affairs were similar to gang rumbles without the Saturday night specials. There might be a dozen kids per side. It was a disorganized scramble, but because it was such a melee, individual flaws didn't stand out (like the fact that I didn't have any idea what I was supposed to do).

Someone passed me the ball and someone else leaped to guard me. I didn't know what was expected, so I looped a desperation toss to get rid of the ball before something bad happened.

It was a skyhook, reminiscent of vintage Kareem Abdul Jabaar, and it dropped through the net with that unmistakable, brief, sharp ripping sound like someone clearing his throat. "Jesus!" breathed the kid who'd brought me to the gym.

For a shining instant, I was the undisputed king of basketball in Keytesville. Several times that day I heard someone whisper, "You oughta see that new kid shoot!" as eyes slewed toward me.

My reputation lasted until eighth-grade practice later that first day when I proved I could run, but I couldn't hide. Coach Stevenson possibly thought I was faking ineptitude, like a traveling pool shark sandbagging small-town hustlers. He had heard the story of my uncanny shot and was puzzled that the run-and-gun phenomenon he'd heard about now couldn't catch the ball except with his nose. But he put me in the team's first game, perhaps believing I was not a practice player but a game player.

I shot at the wrong basket. I forgot the teams switched ends of the court at the half (or I never knew to begin with). I lined up at guard for the center jump, and the second half tipoff came to me. I dropped it, naturally, and had to turn to chase it down. I saw nothing but open court between me and the basket.

I sprinted for a layup. I thought the screams of the fans, my coach, and teammates were encouragement. I rebounded my missed first shot and wondered, in the split second before I put it back up, why a player from the opposing team was blocking out my teammate, who was clawing toward me, his face red and angry.

Fortunately for the team I missed the second shot, too. Unfortunately for me, it established a benchmark against which I was measured for the next five years. I provided lowlights with depressing frequency.

From that dismal moment in the eighth grade until Dud Hayes, the president of the school board, handed me my diploma with a noticeable expression of relief five years later, my basketball career included: *(a)* Shooting and missing a left-handed shot when, as our high school coach and school superintendent Mr. Sadler sourly explained to me as he plunked my ass on the bench, "you can't even make the damn things right-handed"; *(b)* Getting a technical foul when I curled fetally around the ball during a scramble for possession and refused to give it up—even to the referee, who finally tired of my kicking at him and blew the whistle; *(c)* Developing an agonizing case of diarrhea in the middle of a game, the outcome of which is fit only for discussion with a therapist; and *(d)* Making an errant pass that allowed the winning basket by the opposition in a sudden-death double-overtime game. "Maybe Joe made the bad pass we all noticed," Mr. Sadler said at Monday practice. "But you all made mistakes at other times in the game that were just as costly." Even I didn't believe that one.

Basketball was religion in Keytesville, a town that had little past, not much present, and no future. There was an excitement in the tiny little gymnasium, hazy with smoke leaking in from the cigarette-puffing bean farmers in the tiny vestibule.

Our Keytesville home crowd was rural. Many of the men wore overalls. They had quit farm chores a little early so they could bathe and shave for the big occasion. Their ruddy, lined faces were razor-nicked. Shaving was a sometime thing and they weren't good at it. They had eyes reddened from harsh winter wind and field dust. Their hair was home-cut, like a badly mowed hayfield.

The basketball game was as much a social occasion as church or a pie supper. It was a chance to see neighbors and join in a common cause, the downfall of Glasgow or Mendon or Brunswick.

The gym was a vortex that gathered the collective tiny excitements of Keytesville Tiger fans on Friday night. For two hours, Keytesville was a festival, a celebration. Then it was back to snot-nosed cows and numb fingers and shit on old, cold rubber boots. Basketball was the hour of church that comforts, except it was two hours of forgetfulness, even when we lost, which wasn't often. Keytesville's Tigers were aptly named for the last two years of my high school. We were tough, and we were the town's darlings.

A fundamentalist preacher handling rattlesnakes and speaking in tongues didn't have a patch on a red-necked Keytesville rooter speaking a somewhat different tongue to a referee, but also invoking the wrath of God. They expected us to win and we came through Friday after Friday. Only Fayette, with its Neanderthal, glandularly afflicted giants, was able to defuse us.

Chuck Denny, the Fayette star who went on to play center at the University of Missouri, was six foot, five inches tall. He probably couldn't make a college team today because he wasn't agile enough—today he'd have to play guard, and a six-five guard that moves like a seven-two center isn't going to make the cut. But he was Goliath in 1950s basketball.

Denny was blue-collar mean, elbows of iron, fingers of steel. We clung all over him, like a plague of leeches, and he shrugged us off and scored at will. Inevitably the ball went in to him, and the entire Tiger team collapsed on him like a folding umbrella. Today's center would kick it out to someone who would shoot a short jumper. Denny didn't bother with such subtleties. He just sprayed Keytesville players over half the court and laid in two more points. Rarely did the referees call him for fouls. I think they were afraid of him. So Fayette beat us three or four times and kept us out of the state tournament.

I was the quintessential benchwarmer. No one should want anything as much as I wanted to be a starter. It is a debilitating affliction, more enduring than rheumatic fever. All you have to worry about with rheumatic fever is dying; not whether you're going to start on Friday night.

Mr. Sadler issued practice basketballs to his squad, scuffed surplus that had been replaced by new balls. The probable starters got balls that were round, bounced true, and showed minimal wear. He gave me a ball with a ripped seam. Its rubber bladder pouched out like an inguinal hernia. Gerald Linneman and Mr. Sadler's son, Foster, who was my best friend, had truly round basketballs, as did George Hughes and several others—in fact, all others.

I tried to convince myself that Foster got his round ball because he was the coach's son, but I couldn't make that stick. He was tall and agile and he could hit a fifteen-foot left-handed jumper every time.

He simply was a better basketball player than I was—as were Gerald and George and the rest of the round-ball crowd. But I figured it was a simple matter of time and development, so I resolved to work harder than anyone. Former Los Angeles Laker immortal Jerry West learned to dribble by setting up a forest of chairs at odd angles.

I created the same arrangement on the veranda of the Dalton Hotel, my practice court. The veranda was a flimsy assort-

Foster wasn't tall by today's standards, but he was the tallest we had, so he jumped center. Here, he outjumps some forgotten opponent whom we no doubt beat.

ment of ill-laid boards that rattled and shivered as I dribbled the length of the thing.

It was as rickety as a country bridge. It sloped toward the street, indicating imminent collapse. When I dribbled down its length, the structure shuddered and groaned like a dog passing peach pits.

I practiced faking one way, then going the other way around the chairs. Often, I would lose control of the ball, which would bounce over the railing onto the sidewalk below. Passersby learned to detour into the street when they heard the labored pounding from above. More than one feed truck from the Dalton elevator had to stop while I retrieved my errant and crippled basketball from the middle of the dusty road.

Somehow I never achieved the results that Jerry West did. My father breathed heavily of the dusty Dalton air, through tight lips, wondering when the porch was going to topple into the street. Finally he scrounged several boards at a sawmill (maybe ours). "We're going to build a backboard so you can practice somewhere else," he said.

He chose the top of the backyard, which sloped fifteen to twenty degrees toward the street. It never occurred to either one of us to level the court before we put up the backboard, so when we moved dirt from the uphill side to the downhill side, the court was about six inches lower than when we fixed the backboard. Instead of a rim ten feet above the "floor," we had one a half-foot higher.

I think maybe your importance to the 1951–1952 Keytesville Tigers was measured by how close physically you were to the coach, Mr. Sadler. Here, I am at the far end of the front row as he diagrams a play that I will not participate in. Foster (center), Donald Gheens (left), and Gail Friesz (right) all have basketballs . . . without big lumps sticking out of them.

My father scrounged several boards at a sawmill for the backboard. They were fresh-cut oak with inherent problems that didn't surface until we built the backboard. As it dries, green oak contorts as if in the throes of gastritis. The boards began to cup and shrink. Once warped, oak never will straighten. So, the backboard played like a pinball machine. As if it weren't bad enough to have a basketball with a hernia, I also had a backboard with ridges and irruptions that guaranteed an unpredictable carom even with a perfectly round ball.

While the Tigers who lived near Keytesville could go to the open gym and practice, I was shooting at a rim six inches too high on a tiny, sloping dirt court with a herniated basketball. The lopsided ball unerringly exploded off the rim just out of my reach, then bounded downhill.

My father believed I was learning basketball. Actually I was learning to swear like a drill sergeant and to bound down uneven slopes like a Dall sheep—neither talent being useful as a member of the Keytesville Tigers.

I kept at it because I knew that if Mr. Sadler would just put me in a game and let me play I would coalesce hard-learned dribbling skills from the veranda, and shooting skills from the ten-and-a-half-foot rim, and leave Tiger fans gape-mouthed with admiration.

If I gained anything from my hillside court and errant basketball, it was superb conditioning. Fitness was my only weapon on a real basketball court, where I simply ran players down and took the ball away from them. It was a source of amazement and amusement for my teammates who thought I was crazy. No one wanted to play against me in practice games because I was so frenzied that it spooked them. I was a swarm of bees, a fighting tomcat. I just wasn't very good as a basketball player.

Ours was a grimy and seedy school of the 1950s that bore its unremarkable history with weary resignation, like a plow horse wearing an old harness. The architecture was Depression Utility, no gingerbread, just ugly dark red bricks patiently piled one on the other until they made a small-town school. The small gym was dimly lit, with fold-down bleachers along one wall and a stage at the other side. There was no out-of-bounds. You shot a layup and hit the wall a microsecond later. The protective mats were as thin and unresiliant as Rye Krisp.

We usually played in gyms just as idiosyncratic as ours. Some had quirks that made them dangerous. Brookfield's baskets were fastened directly to the wall, even closer than ours. Again, there was no out-of-bounds; players rebounded off the wall like pool balls. Glasgow's floor was on the auditorium stage, and an enthusiastic player, leaping for a runaway ball, risked soaring off into the orchestra pit like Peter Pan, only less aerodynamically.

New Franklin was an anomaly, with a spacious, brightly lit fieldhouse. Visiting players, accustomed to their piano-crate gyms, walked into the New Franklin gym with their hick mouths hanging open. The floor was light blond, opposed to our old-varnish orange, and there was a muted sound even with crowd noise at full throttle. The roar rose into the lofty rafters and vanished.

The New Franklin tournament was a highlight, a chance to play two or three games in a real gym where the lights were bright enough that you could see what you were doing. In 1951, our senior season, I was shooting layups in the pregame warm-up when the New Franklin pep squad cheered for me. Annette and Janette Harris were twin cheerleaders, petite and cute in their little blue-and-white outfits. I noticed them, of course—everybody did. But as we warmed up for the game with the Bulldogs, I studiously avoided gawping at them . . .

We called Gerald Linneman "Trigger" because of his frequent, quick shots. But he made most of them, like this corner jumper. Foster (number 15) moves in for an unlikely rebound.

until they led the squad in a cheer: "Yay! Rah! Number 24!" It rang through the gym like the national anthem, and everyone looked to see who number 24 was, including me. No one seemed to be wearing that number and then I realized that everyone, including Mr. Sadler, was looking at me. I bent my neck painfully and, sure enough, there were the fateful numerals on my jersey.

"Why are they cheering for you?" Mr. Sadler asked. He'd already seen me shoot at the opposing team's basket. He had a right to ask.

"I don't know," I said. In high school I had a looping hair wave like a tsunami, carefully held in place with copious slatherings of Brilliantine. Maybe it was the hairdo—everyone else had a crew cut.

A year later, in college, I asked one of the twins why they'd done that. It took a while for her to remember, and then she said offhandedly, "I don't know—I guess we thought you were cute."

9

The Game of Summer

Baseball was a game of grace and skill that could be played by anyone. Size was no barrier. You could be a shrimp short-stop or a mammoth first baseman. You could be as quick as a ground-eating second baseman or as slow as a lumbering catcher. It was the universal game, the American Pastime. We all played it.

It took only one imaginative kid to play baseball in those days. I could become a catcher circling under a pop-up by throwing the ball straight up. Or I could lob a high arcing throw and race under it to make an over-the-shoulder catch like the one that Al Gionfriddo made to rob Joe Dimaggio of a home run in the 1947 World Series.

Or I could find an agreeable wall and bounce grounders off it. Baseballs were expensive and quickly abraded by concrete and brick, so a tennis ball worked better for wall grounders—and hurt a hell of a lot less when I misjudged a short-hopper and it hit me in the throat.

Two boys composed a competitive game. We could play burn-out or pitcher-catcher or pitch-bunt or take turns lofting fly balls or hitting grounders. The variations were almost endless.

Summer was a dreamy time, unmarred by today's distractions. There was no television; only radio, which was best late in the evening when it was too dark to see a dirty baseball. There were no malls to cruise, no organized games. We organized our own games and they were shrill with recrimination and accusation. Sometimes they ended abruptly when the owner of the baseball got huffy and went home with the ball, but mostly they were amiably contentious.

When we moved to Missouri, I found that baseball was secondary to basketball, but still ruled in the summer.

My buddies in Chicago, Gust Dickett and Bob Zahorik, vanished into history, and Karl Miller, who lived on a farm three miles from Dalton, and Foster Sadler, who lived six miles away in Keytesville, became my new best friends.

Karl and I always had our ball gloves. Foster, a far better athlete, was busy playing American Legion baseball while Karl and I played catch and hoped for a pickup game with other middling ballplayers.

I spent twenty-five dollars for a Wilson fielder's glove, equivalent to a hundred-dollar or more investment today. The rich leather shone with oiled opulence. This was a *glove!* Better company a teenage baseball player never had. My ball glove was my pet. I wouldn't have spent five seconds taking care of shoe leather, but I endlessly kneaded saddle soap into the pocket of my baseball glove. I slathered leather dressing on my left hand and worked it throughout the inside of the glove. It was part of me. When I wasn't wearing it, I stowed it carefully cradling a baseball, to shape the pocket.

I was Marty Marion, Red Schoendienst, with this glove. I could do no wrong. I rotated between second and first or between second and third (depending on how desperate the coach was on a given game day) and smacked my right fist into this lovely glove and felt whole, complete, as if a part long missing had been restored to me.

Someone stole the glove when I was in college. It vanished from my room and I never had a clue as to where it went. And something went out of baseball, as if an outfield floodlight had shorted and exploded, leaving the field in half-light.

In high school, I swung a Larry Doby bat, dimly aware that the Cleveland star was black—in fact, the first American League black player and only the second in the majors after Jackie Robinson. I used his bat because it felt good, not because I was making a racial statement.

I used that bat to hit the only home run of my career. The Keytesville Cookies were playing at Glasgow where my great-grandfather had gotten himself captured by the Confederates. I hit a line drive that got past the left fielder and rolled over the bank into the dense vegetation on the banks of the Missouri River, and no one could find it as I circled the bases.

We had to call the game because it was the only game ball.

As a baseball player, I had fair fielding ability, an inconsistent bat, and quickness. I could get to any ball, but it was questionable whether I could field it or not. Yet my throwing arm was good, and I was the pitcher when Foster needed to rest his arm.

As a pitcher I was Mr. Sadler's despair. I could throw every known pitch, including a knuckleball. My curve dropped sharply and I could even throw a screwball, a reverse curve. I had a good change-up that floated up to the plate like a balloon after a sharp fastball. There was just one niggling problem: I didn't have any idea where the ball was going when I released it. I hit batters, I threw in the dirt, I threw ten feet over the catcher's head. Once I had a no-hitter going into the seventh inning . . . but we were behind 4-1 because I had walked in four runs.

Mr. Sadler would shake his head and look up and down the bench for relief, but there was none. As bad as I was, I was better than the others.

My hitting was as inconsistent as my pitching—as a high school senior I batted .177 with three hits in eighteen at-bats. Hustle was much of what I had going for me. I tried to make up for my pitiful hitting with hard running on dribblers to the infield and sometimes beat them out for hits that looked as impressive in the box score as a screaming liner.

My fielding was so-so. Pretty good outfielder, with range and fair hands and a fair arm. With that magic glove, I was better than I should have been.

A ball glove was a working icon. It was more than a tool. It was an extension of the body, as natural as fingernails and hair. It was a mostly constant companion during the clement months. When it turned cold and baseball season ended, I'd carefully rub neat's-foot oil into the pocket of the glove, wrap it once more around a baseball, then carefully store it in my bedroom, as if preserving the bones of a saint.

My first glove had been that enormous catcher's mitt, a huge, circular glove with a pocket precisely the size of a baseball, surrounded by a pillow of padding. Maybe there was some prescient element in my father's choice of a catcher's mitt, because I did become a catcher in high school. I was the only one stupid enough to squat before Foster's wicked curves and whistling fastball. Foster was left-handed, which meant his curve broke in to a right-handed batter, a dirty trick to pull on a high school kid.

His fastball seemed to hiss with speed to us, though it probably wasn't all that fast. Still, it was faster than anything we threw and hard to catch because it always had a "hop," the illusionary change of speed that happens when the ball nears the

How do I always get so far away from Mr. Sadler? I'm leaning, second from left, front row, on the Larry Doby bat, which might have made a racial statement, but certainly didn't make much of one in the statistics. Foster is the only one wearing a jacket, to protect his precious pitching arm, while Karl stands to his left, elbow akimbo, confident that his next at-bat will lift him above the .200 mark.

plate (actually it's a slight change of direction, a minicurve, but it looks like the ball shifts gears and steps on the gas).

Foster and I became more than battery mates; we became best friends. I'm not sure how the chemistry of friendship works, but I decided early on, after we moved to Dalton, that I wanted him to be my friend. He was the most popular boy in school.

It had nothing to do with the fact that his father was the school superintendent and coach, or that his mother was the school secretary. Foster was smarter than any boy in school, but didn't flaunt it. He was tall and lean, with a country face, like Chet Atkins, or Jimmy Dean of sausage fame.

He was, as far as I can remember, the only left-handed kid in school, certainly the only port-sided athlete. That made him both an anomaly and a curiosity. Since there were so few left-handers, he had an advantage in basketball and baseball: Those guarding him in basketball weren't ready for a left-handed shot, and those he pitched against in baseball couldn't cope with a ball that did things the reverse of what they were used to.

Foster's folks became surrogate parents for me. His father was stocky and swarthy, with piercing eyes and a commanding presence. He was approachable and friendly, but also stern. He would take off his shirt, revealing an old-style sleeveless undershirt, and scrimmage with us on the basketball court.

There was no quarter given in those games. He was competitive and expected his boys to be the same. Once I guarded him and he nearly broke my arm slapping at the ball. He was as hard as granite, and we alternated between fear and respect—fear of discovery, if we'd done something wrong, and respect, always.

There were horror stories of Mr. Sadler wielding the flat paddle he reputedly kept behind his desk, though I never got a whipping, nor knew for certain that anyone else did. The threat was enough to keep kids straight.

"Straight" was light years from today. There were no drugs, save the occasional kid who drank beer. The ultimate drug abuse was a half-pint of Four Roses, split between three or four senior boys. Many kids smoked, but always on the sly. Get caught with a cigarette on school grounds and it was a dozen whacks with the paddle, or so we believed.

Not one girl in my four years of high school got pregnant. It wasn't that everyone was chaste; it was that they either were careful, lucky, or used condoms—almost certainly the last. Any boy unlucky enough to get a girl pregnant was expected to marry her, and I'm sure that happened. There was the occasional "premature" baby, but not many.

Foster, Karl, and I once went to a roadhouse near Salisbury in a pickup truck belonging to Karl's father. We got a friend to buy us a six-pack of Griesedieck, and we found a pulloff in a field and each drank two beers while we talked about life.

None of it was about sex experience, since we didn't have any—at least Karl and I didn't. If Foster, who dated often, had anything to tell, he wouldn't have. Foster was a private person who never confessed dreams or problems. He would stick with the easy topics, keeping the rest to himself.

We respected each other's turf. Foster was determined to go as far as he could in sports, but he figured he had a better chance at a small school, so planned to go to Central Methodist College, a few miles south at Fayette.

There was no choice for me. I wanted to be a writer, and the University of Missouri had one of the top several journalism schools in the country. Karl, a year behind in high school, still was uncertain. He didn't want to farm, and neither did I, which I'm sure caused our fathers some bleak moments.

Karl was stocky and just short of clumsy. Once he slapped a single into right field, which the right fielder bobbled. Karl rounded first base and headed for second. He and the ball arrived at the same time. He should have slid, but instead his spikes caught and he stumbled comically across second base into the outfield, where the second baseman easily tagged him.

Of course the entire team ragged him unmercifully, including me. Karl said nothing, sat on the bench, with the eyes of the small crowd burning the back of his neck, the taunts of his teammates burning the rest of him. It wasn't until later—too much later—that I put myself in his place and realized how much we had humiliated him.

Karl was vulnerable and Foster was not. It wouldn't have occurred to anyone to jeer at Foster, even assuming he made a mistake in the first place. He was a leader, and Karl and I were followers.

We headed home after we finished our beers, feeling the tiniest of buzzes, and when we got to Sadler's and Foster opened the passenger door, a couple of empty bottles clattered out on the pavement and rolled into the ditch.

It was dead silent in Keytesville; the town was shut down for the night. We were terrified. Had Mr. Sadler heard those bottles hit the road? Would the lights come on, first in the house, then on the porch? Would that blocky, unyielding figure stand in silhouette and demand an accounting?

For an agonizingly long time we held our breath. Nothing stirred, and we carefully let our breath out; Foster even more carefully picked up the two bottles and placed them back in the truck as if they were filled with nitroglycerine. "See you tomorrow," he said, easing the door closed. We winced when it clicked, and Karl said, "Whew!"

We formed a town team called the Keytesville Cookies. Basically, it was the players not good enough to make the Salisbury Legion team, which meant Foster and Gerald Linneman weren't on it. And that meant I got to pitch, to get out from behind that mask and from behind the plate.

Now I was on the pitcher's mound, that almost imperceptible elevation that puts the pitcher above everyone else. He is King of the Hill. I was glad to quit catching, at least for the Cookies' season. During the final game of the high school season, Foster had skipped an errant fastball off the dirt in front of the plate, and it bounced under my glove and hit me in the balls. I scrabbled around in the dust of home plate, clutching my knee, because you simply didn't grab your testicles in front of a crowd.

Catching is a good way to get hurt. In that same game, a burly player from Brunswick charged home from third base, trying to score. The throw in beat him by a mile, and I clasped the ball to my bosom and shut my eyes. He didn't bother to slide; he just hit me like Jim Brown going off tackle, and I landed near the backstop, stunned and bruised . . . but with the ball still in my glove.

Injury, or the potential for it, wasn't limited to catching. Once I tried to score from third base on what they call a suicide squeeze. You race for home plate with the pitch and the batter is supposed to lay down a bunt. Instead, Lloyd Kalinka— "Clinky," as we called him—swung away and laced a vicious line drive past my ear at a distance of about fifteen feet. The ball hissed by like a rifle bullet. I tottered weakly the rest of the way home to score and then sat on the bench breathing deeply for a long time. "I didn't get the signal," Clinky said apologetically.

Keytesville's baseball field was a place as quirky as its basketball court. Bobby Cunningham fell into a drain culvert in center field as he circled under a fly ball. He vanished from sight and we thought perhaps he had been swallowed by the earth, but he presently clambered out of the hole and chased the ball down, too late to prevent an inside-the-park homer.

The summer between our junior and senior years, the Cookies played a game that also served as a forum for local political candidates to make speeches. The game came after the speeches. The speakers stood at home plate, talking through the screen to the crowd in the stands. It got later and later, and we grew more restless.

Finally Karl and I began to play catch along the third-base line. Karl threw wildly and the ball sailed toward the backstop, bounced off and came to rest at the feet of the candidate for county assessor. "'Scuze me," I muttered, picking up the ball. I motioned to Karl that we should swap positions so that I would be throwing toward the plate. And of course I let one get away from me, a hummer that sailed over Karl's head, over the speaker's head, and rattled off the backstop.

The Cookies had uniforms of an ugly sandy color, as if they'd been laundered in the Missouri River, and none of them fit. Our team had the life of a mayfly, a brief summer fling, quickly over. A few games one summer between our junior and senior years, and the Cookies were history.

A few years ago, Karl and I got together for dinner and, in the manner of old friends who have not seen each other for many years, searched for common ground.

That, of course, would have been baseball. We spoke simultaneously, each echoing the other. "Since the strike, I gave it up."

10

The Nazi and the Hell Machine

Most kids I knew had summer jobs when they hit teenager-hood. Me? I lay around like an indolent playboy, wearing my cast-off silk robe/smoking jacket (and sneaking off to the out-house for the actual smoking), listening to Bessie Smith records, and dreading the next skin eruption.

It wasn't that I didn't want to work; it was that I was inca-pable of what is generally considered productive effort—any-thing I knew how to do, no one wanted. I weighed 115 pounds and could barely lift a bale of hay, much less pitch it to the top of a stack.

I couldn't drive a truck or a tractor—I had already demon-strated my driving ability by denting Raymond Ross's truck. I put in a brief stint as a gofer at the B & J Grocery, one of two grocery stores in Dalton. Bread was fourteen cents a loaf and cigarettes seventeen cents a pack. Except in dire emergency, Bea and Jay, the owners, kept me away from the frightening task of making change.

My job was to fetch jugs of "coal oil" for lamps from the kerosene barrel in the back. Most of the customers who bought it were black and had no electricity. They used corncobs to stopper their jugs. My stint at the grocery store didn't last long, and then I was looking for another job.

There was one job that I could do, simply because not only could anyone do it, no one wanted to. If you were outside the cemetery gates, you were eligible to detassel seed corn. The mere mention of the word *detassel* makes me quiver uneasily, as if the Hell Machine had rumbled past once again.

Detasseling is necessary so corn will hybridize. Crossing two varieties brings out the best in each. Hybrids grow with more vigor than regular plants. First, plant six "cow rows," corn of one variety, and two "bull rows," corn of another variety.

Then, in order to cross-pollinate, you must eliminate pollen from the lady rows so they are pollinated only by their bullish neighbors. The cow ears will produce the hybrid seed. As the cow corn grows, it proffers tassels to the sun. Detasselers must eliminate the sexual plumes of the cow rows, which leaves the standing stalks lasciviously waiting for the gentle fall of yellow bull-row pollen. It sounds absolutely wanton, and maybe it is to a cornstalk, but it was hell on the sinuses of a kid with hay fever.

Had Dante Alighieri been a Midwestern row-crop farmer when he wrote the *Divine Comedy,* he would have substituted an endless row of seed corn for the souls of the damned to de-tassel eternally instead of the sea of ice at the pit of hell. As quickly as they pulled a sticky tassel, a new one would sprout. Detasselers would pull and pull in blinding heat, sweat pouring off them, muscles cramping, never quite catching up, plagued by thirst and hunger, always a half-row away from a drink of water and twenty minutes from lunch, reviled by a sneering foredemon.

Occasionally, the foredemon would call a lunch break and the damned souls would fall on their sack lunches with glad cries, only to find a baloney sandwich, a warm Big Orange, and a Moon Pie. People in hell eat that lunch. Every damned day.

So, I got a job detasseling seed corn because I was desperate. The field boss looked at me and muttered, "Scrawny little bastard, ain't you. Hope to hell you can keep up. We don't need no pusses out there."

The detasseling machine consisted of four platforms, suspended from a pipe steel framework built around a wheeled vehicle. The driver sat far above the platforms and the machine extended over the six cow rows. Two detasselers were on each twelve-inch platform, with a safety bar about waist high.

The detasseler in front worked two rows, the one behind picked up tassels that were missed. We took turns in the front position because tassels simply came too fast to keep up. I often had a helpless feeling, pulling tassels frenziedly, sweating and itching from the pollen, sticky with corn sap, no chance to rest or scratch until the turnaround (which came seldom because the rows were a half mile or more long).

I was little, but quick. My hands were a blur and I danced on the detasseling machine platform like Fred Astaire. I set about detasseling with grim determination. I worked as if possessed.

Except nobody cared. If I wanted to work hard, do the work of two detasselers, fine, one of the others would hang loose. It took me most of the summer to realize no one appreciated hard work.

This was a revelation, because I'd been brought up to believe that hard work inevitably brings reward. My parents believed this and told me so. It had worked for them—they'd left humble beginnings and done well. They didn't care what I did, but urged me to do more than was asked and I would be rewarded.

So I detasseled harder than anyone and found that detasseling was not the stuff of a Horatio Alger book. No Daddy Warbucks would appear to take me in hand and make me a prince. My hard work was merely the foundation for more hard work.

We rode to and from the fields in the back of a flatbed truck with nothing between us and the gravel road except our ability to cling to the jouncing truck. Detasseling in the days before workers' rights, Porta-Potties in the field, and minimum wage was not far removed from working on a Georgia chain gang. I made five dollars for a ten-hour day. Five dollars a day was a fortune to me.

I was setting aside money for one thing, not a date, nor new blue jeans. I wanted a guitar—specifically, a Martin guitar. My first guitar had been a Sears Silvertone f-hole guitar with an action so high that King Kong couldn't have pressed the strings to the fingerboard. My fingers, no matter how conditioned, hurt as if they'd been hammered with a splitting maul every time I played that clunky thing.

It wasn't a guitar; it was punishment. I saw photos of Hank Williams and Ernest Tubb and Hank Snow and every one of them had a guitar with the "C. F. Martin" logo on the peghead. My fantasy was that the only thing between me and the Grand Ol' Opry was the lack of a suitable musical instrument.

The guitar gave purpose to the long summer. It was my Grail. I didn't care about being a wage-earning, productive member of society. I just wanted a Martin. When I flexed my aching fingers to pull yet another corn tassel, I told myself I was strengthening them for an F-7th chord. And at the end of each ten-hour day, I was five dollars closer to my Martin.

The field boss would show up about once a day and confer briefly with the detasseling machine driver to make sure no one was creating unrest, then he would speed off in a cloud of Missouri River–bottom dust. He didn't fraternize with the field hands. No "Hey, how yah doin'?" and no "You guys need anything?"

So, I made my five dollars a day and my folks were impressed. The son they thought never would amount to a hill of corn was earning a salary working among hills of corn. I was getting an actual check each Friday, far less, but similar in appearance to those my father had gotten before he chucked it all to join the landed gentry.

Actually, his income in 1951 was less visible than mine. His money came and went fitfully, the "went" with startling rapidity—the bank owned us, save for that creaking old hotel, which no bank in its right mind would have wanted. Every cent not necessary for bare maintenance went to retiring the debt on the land my father and his partners owned. The golden flow of beans and corn from the harvester into the wagon translated into cash that flowed into the vault at Salisbury Savings Bank.

When the augur spout spewed a molten flow of grain into the truck, you could stick your hand into it, feel the abrasive bite of the falling kernels, and maybe come away with a slim handful of corn or beans. Similarly, my father stuck his hand in the cash flow from the farm, and what little stuck to it was what we lived on.

Detasseling was brutal, unending work, supervised by a little German man who was gnomish, malevolent of expression. He had long yellow horse-teeth and an oozing facial sore.

He snarled at us in heavily accented English. This was only a few years beyond World War II. We knew he wasn't a Nazi. He'd been raised in Dalton and his family probably was part of a mid-1800s German migration to the Missouri River corridor. But it didn't matter. The whole country held a residual animosity toward Germans, especially ones who snapped at you for missing tassels.

The facial sore probably was skin cancer, although I thought it was his basic meanness leaking out. He drove the detaseling machine as if it were an engine of war.

I called him the Nazi, though not to his face. The Nazi delighted in driving just too fast for us to keep up with the unending tassels, then chewing us out for missing some, muttering harsh, unintelligible threats.

At the time, sweating, itchy, and sticky with pollen, bone-tired, I hated him. But I suspect he was merely a poor, sick little man with a dying face, scared of dying, in 105-degree temperatures.

The heat was intolerable—1951 was among the hottest years in modern times, the hottest since the year I was born. Sun baked the Dalton bottoms and the corn slumped limply in the unremitting heat. But corn detasseling went on, rain, shine, or throbbing heat.

Late one afternoon in the cornfield I began to feel strange. I lost my energy, felt sick to my stomach, and simply could not go on. We had perhaps one round to make before quitting time. "Come on!" demanded the driver. "One more round. Anybody can do that." But I couldn't. I was sick.

He turned away, disgusted, and the machine vanished in the tall, green corn, its sound gradually muffled, then lost. I slumped at the end of the corn rows, ashamed of my weakness on one hand, too sick to care on the other. I didn't know if I was more ashamed or sick.

Finally the machine returned, the detasselers looking curiously at me, as they would at a dog that had been run over but was still alive.

The field boss arrived in his dusty pickup, got out, and asked the Nazi why I was sitting in the slim shade of a locust sprout. "Ah, he says he's sick," the Nazi grumbled.

"We're not payin' yuh to sit on your ass, yuh know," said the field boss.

Had the Angel Michael appeared at that moment, offered me his gleaming sword, and said, "Joel, we've been watching you Upstairs and we think you have promise. You have a choice: take this sword and slice that sucker long and deep . . . or sit here in the shade like a wimp," I would have waved off the sword and tried not to vomit on the Man's shoes.

I rode home in the rattling flatbed truck and I told my folks what had happened. By then I was running a fever and was becoming incoherent. It all seemed like a bad dream, one of those childhood tonsil nightmares with the big, soft cubes softly crushing out my life.

"Well, you're not going back out there!" my mother declared. She almost never got upset about anything, but this was different. She was ready to take on the seed corn company and the Nazi and anyone else who had harmed her chick.

Her chick, meanwhile, was absolutely delighted to be relieved of frontline duty. I was ready for R and R. Summer was for baseball, not facilitating the mating of cornstalks.

I never went back. That was the end of my detasseling career.

I bought the Martin from Lyon & Healey in Chicago. It was a mahogany-topped 00-17 model that cost sixty dollars then and is worth about a thousand dollars now.

Years later I found that my enduring hero, Jimmie Rodgers, began his career with a 00-17 Martin. There is a seamless unity to this, as if perhaps the Angel Michael reported to his Boss, "Well, he didn't want the sword," and the Boss said, "Ah, give him a Martin, like that yodeler from the thirties. Maybe something will come of it."

I've been waiting ever since for something to come of it.

11

Dating in the Dark Ages

Everyone has someone they worshiped in the painful teenage years, someone unattainable. My dream girl was Marleen Brown.

She had eyes that flashed, a dimpled smile, and soft dark hair that draped across her shoulders. Her cheeks bloomed. It always was spring on her face.

She was a little bit of everything at Keytesville High School—class officer, Barnwarming queen, pep-squad cheerleader, editor of the yearbook, and member of both the student council and the glee club.

And she was going steady with a West Point cadet, a fellow who had graduated two years ahead of us. So all I could do was gawp in helpless puppy love. I could only mumble and stumble and act the fool around her. There I was, six miles from town and a dozen from where Marleen lived; I didn't have a car, didn't have any money, and knew nothing about talking to girls. I had the savoir faire of a tuna fish. Car or no car, it would have made no difference because Marleen didn't date anyone except her cadet.

I was unsure and intimidated by all girls, but especially by

Marleen because she was the most beautiful girl in school and because she was unofficially engaged to the cadet. A girl who was going steady was off limits to any but the most bold, and a girl who was unofficially engaged, especially to a West Point cadet (a unique situation at Keytesville High School), was completely out of reach.

So all I could do was dream my incomplete little dreams and sigh for what could not have been. Besides, I figured that if I even acted as if I were pursuing Marleen, her cadet would come home from the military academy armed with the weapons of modern warfare and make me a bit of military history.

In our junior class play, Marleen and I played mischievous twins. It was a typically stupid Keytesville production. Kids today mount elaborate costumed productions of *South Pacific,* but we put on *The Daffy Dills,* a silly comedy written by the dramatic equivalent of Clem Kadiddlehopper.

Marleen's costume was a little-girl dress that was about one size too small and made my mouth go dry. I'm sure Marleen knew that I was dumbstruck over her since I spent most of my time around her blushing and gulping. When I could forget that I was hopelessly in love with her, we had fun and made a perfect pair, both small and petite.

She kissed me backstage one night at practice. We were talking and no one was around and I was blushing and stammering and she stepped close to me and kissed me.

Maybe she was practicing her womanly skills. Maybe she felt sorry for me. Maybe she just felt like kissing someone, and I was a handy target. But she gave me something to dream on before we turned in different directions.

Our senior yearbook was called *The Regit,* which is "Tiger" spelled backward, a really dumb idea, but better than the previous year's book, which was the *Tiger Folleader,* an awful conjoining of *follower* and *leader.*

Marleen and I played the Daffy Dill twins, a play so dumb that the Three Stooges would have rejected it.

Marleen's photo is first among the seniors. She is looking back over her shoulder, as if someone she cherishes had just called to her from behind. Perhaps it was me, but I doubt it. More likely it was her mother saying that her cadet was telephoning from West Point.

I'm at the lower right-hand corner of the page, Marleen at the upper left. If it were me she were looking for, she would be looking slightly down. No, it probably was the cadet.

I suspect being infatuated with Marleen actually inhibited my dating. It would have been like cheating on her if I dated anyone else, a stupidly romantic attitude that penalized my social life. Marleen didn't care if I dated others or not; it was just my knotty romanticism that got in the way.

Still, I did have the occasional date, and dating was a trau-

In the yearbook, Marleen is looking over her shoulder, but not at me; I'm down the page, as far from her in photos as I was in life.

matic affair in the 1950s; it was just slightly tougher than Marine boot camp. Or at least it was for me, with no experience, no self-confidence, and the handicaps of living in a backwater with limited resources.

When we moved to Dalton from Chicago in the late 1940s, I was at first considered a sophisticate. I was the only big-city kid in school, something of a curiosity, like the German exchange student.

But after my first official date with a farm girl, the girl confided to a friend, who then took great pleasure in telling me that I was "as green as grass."

And here I'd thought of myself as somewhat suave, perhaps even debonair. I could play the guitar and knew well-known love songs like "The Drunkard's Daughter." I could sing "The Wreck on the Highway" just like Roy Acuff ("Ah saw the blood on the highway / But Ah didn't hear nobody pray"). Such talent should have had rural Missouri girls falling all over me. What more could a farmer's daughter want than a barely post-adolescent Ernest Tubb?

There seemed to be a culture warp in operation. Farm kids, who logically should have been listening to Hank Snow, instead danced to Frank Sinatra. Boys who slopped hogs no more would have been caught listening to Webb Pierce than they would have been caught molesting the sheep. They felt that anyone who tuned in the Grand Ol' Opry doubtless also dated young female pigs on a regular basis.

During my teenage years, I was enamored of the novels of Thorne Smith. Smith, now largely forgotten, was a phenomenon of the 1920s. Born in 1893, he served in the navy during World War I, but after, wrote *Topper* and many other novels then considered risqué, now merely sophomorically silly. Lissome women ran around in their "step-ins" (panties, presumably sheer and with lace and probably black), and nearly constant sex was implied, but never spelled out. I don't remember his characters hugging or kissing, never mind caressing a creamy thigh. They just scampered around in step-ins with much drinking and implicit wild behavior.

I'd never seen a girl in or out of step-ins, except once when my father and I drove down to the country store at Guilford's Ford and a Guilford girl ran across the front yard and behind the house in her underwear.

Her underbritches were homemade stuff, probably from flour sacks, and were as far from step-ins as Elizabeth Taylor pearls are from strung popcorn. It was not Victoria's Secret incarnate. Still, it was a magic moment.

Girls in step-ins were the stuff of my dreams. I couldn't imagine them out of their underwear any more than I could imagine what pâté de fois gras tasted like. My father and I shot Canada geese, but the livers went into the gut bucket and were not processed as pâté.

I huddled in my den in the Dalton Hotel, swathed in my silk robe, and pounded away on a rickety Underwood typewriter that certainly dated from the Thorne Smith era. I wrote Thorne Smith imitations, replete with rowdy women and bibulous men (Smith was a drinker and died of alcoholism the year I was born, 1934).

Writing about sex was a substitute for doing it, though not a very satisfactory one. Still, I was in control of events on the written page, a situation that wasn't true in reality. I could make my female characters pliant and passionate. They were not like the girls I knew, who were neither pliant nor passionate, at least not with me. I heard stories about girls who "went all the way," but they didn't go anywhere with me.

I was afraid of girls, like a stray dog that desperately wants affection but is spooky about asking for it. I would have sooner thought of slugging Mr. Sadler as of laying a sweaty hand on the budding bosom of anyone of feminine persuasion.

Dalton boys didn't date. Karl and I played baseball, picked

Marleen and I are conspiring to take over the student government, but Mr. Sadler, back row left, and Warren Lee, our class advisor, will make sure that doesn't happen. Lennie Johnson, my first girlfriend, is seated left, possibly checking me for impetigo scabs.

up pecans for pocket money, and hunted ducks. Sometimes we set out trot lines at the Cutoff, which invariably were called "trout" lines, even though no one I knew in the 1950s had seen a trout.

Almost no one had a car, but if you lived in Keytesville you could walk to the girl's house, endure a horrible few moments with her twittering mother, or, God forbid, her tight-jawed father, then walk to the drugstore for a soda. Those who lived in a town of size had a pool from which to pick a date, and a choice of a movie theater or soda fountain to visit; in Dalton, there were no more than a couple of eligible dates of either sex and nowhere to go.

I did get a date for the junior-senior prom, and my mother

fussed for a week with my outfit, an ill-fitting sports jacket with pants that high-watered somewhere around my ankles. Since I wasn't quite old enough to drive, my father would have to drive me to the gym, where the prom was, then pick me up at a fixed time. I'd meet my date there.

It would be as arranged as an old-time Spanish wedding, and the odds against any real romance occurring were astronomical. Perhaps I could steal a kiss in a dark corner on the dance floor, if the ever-vigilant chaperons, Mr. Pegler and Miss Gerhardt, weren't prowling nearby.

And then I suffered an attack of impetigo, which left a horrific scab that covered much of my chin, and I knew there wasn't going to be any romance of any kind. Both my quasidate and I were thankful for the romantic gloom of the gym— so she wouldn't have to look at my crusty face, and so I wouldn't have to show it to the world.

A senior, who owned a car, danced with my date and took her home. His car was a Model A Ford, but it was one car more than I had. My father picked me up at the designated time, and I rode home in misery.

Dalton boys talked about girls the way we talked about flying saucers, a popular subject in the 1950s. But most of us never got any more intimate with a girl than we did with a Martian.

Most girls of the 1950s were coy and needed coaxing. You nibbled at her cheek with dry lips, gradually working your way toward her lips. Finally you were in position to kiss, separated by an inch or two of superheated air.

This is when you closed your eyes, not because of passion, but because there was nothing more terrible than seeing the enormous eye of the girl you were kissing as she watched you. The first time this happened, I shut my eyes and plunged recklessly into kissing, as if I were diving into a new swimming hole. And like unknown waters, kissing was studded with stumps and rocks. That first coy girl turned her face just slightly, so my passionate kiss slid sloppily across her cheek. My lips made a horrible slurping sound and I left a wet trail like a garden slug.

Once I was alone with a girl in the wings of the gymnasium stage after school. The subject of French kissing came up. I wasn't sure how to French kiss, but knew that if it was French, it would melt your fingernails.

I made desperate jokes and did my cool impression of Charles Boyer, which was something like Curly Bill of the Three Stooges. The girl was a passionate redhead whose credo was "put up or shut up" and she cut to the chase while I was still babbling my hammy, atrocious line. She grabbed me like a wrestling bear and French kissed me so sloppily that drool ran down my chin.

It was like asking for a dessert and getting hit in the face with a cream pie. I didn't know much, but I couldn't believe really good French kissing involved so much moisture. I don't re-member her name, but I remember her lips with uncanny pre-cision. It was the first time my tongue had touched the mem-branous tissue inside another human's mouth.

She pulled away with the sound of a plumber's friend clear-ing a clogged drain and looked expectantly at me. I stumbled back against the wall, thumping my head, and took a deep, shuddery breath. She mistook that for passion, not apprehen-sion, and sized me up for the next bite. I was scared to death.

It was as if I'd graduated from the first grade into a college honors class. She was teaching the calculus of love and I was still struggling with simple addition. The school bus horn sounded and I mumbled some feeble excuse and fled. It was the only time I ever welcomed that bus signal.

When I reached sixteen, I was old enough to drive, and that's when a long-running skirmish started between my father and me over use of the family car for dating. Our family car was a sedate Ford, already in its declining years. My father used it as a utility vehicle, and the back seat was crammed with buckets of walnuts, farm produce, and greasy tools.

The passenger seat was reserved for the family dog—or my dates. Chaps was a smelly spaniel who was fond of rolling in disgusting substances. The ideal date for me was both broad-minded and suffering from a deep head cold that numbed her sense of smell.

The seat cover generated enough static electricity to light Las Vegas. On one outing I slid suavely across the wide seat to my date's side, reached up to caress her silken cheek, and saw a bright blue spark leap a half-inch from my fingertip to her face. She screamed and recoiled, banging her head painfully on the doorpost, then rebounded forward and we cracked foreheads.

It was our only date.

There was almost no place to go on a date. The nearest movie theater was ten miles away, so I had a minimum of twenty miles invested—roughly a gallon of gas (a quarter's worth). The movie was a buck and a half, plus obligatory Milk Duds and a Coke. I'd already invested two dollars in a date, at least half my usual resources, and hadn't even gotten to the interesting part.

A few times a year there were community social events: box or pie suppers, square dances, or hayrides. The first two were carefully chaperoned and about as much fun as rendering lard, but a hayride promised something different. It was dark and you were recumbent with a live, pulsating girl. The potential was awesome.

I went on one hayride when I was a freshman at Keytesville High School. It was in an iron-tired wagon, drawn by a noisy John Deere tractor.

The night was as dark as a tax collector's heart, and my statuesque blonde was nestled next to me under a scratchy blanket. (This was before our future was clouded by impetigo.) Hayriders were supposed to kiss until their lips chapped, but I was petrified. I was in the long grass with a wounded lion, and my mind kept saying, "you gotta do something!" but my body wouldn't function.

I didn't even nibble an earlobe. I just babbled until she was ready to throw me out of the wagon and demand loudly, "Is there a guy here who knows how to do something with his lips except let them flap all the time?"

Once I had a date with a girl reputed to Go All The Way. She had, by one account, been naked in bed with an upperclassman, and they weren't catching some sun.

She had a forward manner and once, as I sat on a table in the gymnasium vestibule, she marched between my legs, pressed against me, and smiled suggestively. I, of course, muttered some inane comment and managed to chill the magic moment. Still, she agreed to go to the movies in Brunswick with me.

I cleared the passenger seat of the family car of dog hair and rusty tools and off we went. This would, I was sure, be the night when my innocence fled. But like my other fantasies, this one was best experienced before the fact.

A would-be suitor of the girl also was at the El Jon, and he followed us as we left town. My intent was to find a secluded country road (there were a hundred miles of them in Chariton County) and engage in lust.

His intent, however, was to thwart any romantic interludes by following us, his headlights on high beam. We raced through the Dalton bottoms, where you can see for miles. Not much chance of losing a pursuer here. I summarized his ancestry, which included no wedlock.

I tried every trick I could think of: suddenly pulling into a side road and switching off the lights, making a sharp turn and heading the other way. Nothing worked. He stuck with us and he obviously had a bottomless gas tank.

Finally, I pulled into the girl's driveway and shut off the lights. The pursuer had no choice. He parked behind us for a few minutes, revving his engine, the headlights bright through the back window of the Vancemobile.

Then he backed out of the driveway and sped into the night. Finally we were alone, but being alone in her front yard was not the most auspicious place to consummate anything except perhaps a chaste peck on the cheek or maybe a handshake. For all I knew her father was at that moment ramming shotshells into his Sears Autoloader.

"Okay, let's find a dark place and get acquainted," I leered.

"We can't," she said. "Daddy probably heard us come in. We can sit here for a while." Sitting is not what I had in mind. A more recumbent position seemed to offer greater potential. Recumbency was out of the question—if for no other reason than I couldn't see through the windshield. I wanted time to floor the Ford if I saw Daddy crossing the yard.

We kissed a few times, but I'm sure we were both alert for the creak of the screen door; I was positive that at any moment the car door would be yanked open by her father, in a towering rage. He would jerk me from the car with his large farmer hands and rip me into pieces suitable for hog food.

Not only did I not get deflowered that night, but my father, who had filled the gas tank the day before, grumbled, "What did you do, drive to Arizona?"

12

The Making of a Non-Farm Boy

My father was a farmer in the same sense that an infantry general is a foot soldier. Even though his roots were on the farm, his maturation and training were city.

He didn't pine for his city days, as far as I know, but he couldn't have driven a tractor to save his life, nor did he have a feeling for the rhythms of crops and livestock. He was a foreman.

And I knew even less. But my friends were farm kids, and they seemed to associate congenially with sheep and hogs and chickens. So animal husbandry sounded like something I could do. From what little I knew, farm animals pretty well took care of themselves, and then you sold them for big bucks.

So Foster and Tommy Coy and I joined the FFA, Future Farmers of America, whose aim is "development of agricultural leadership, cooperation, and citizenship."

My motives were not to become a successful farmer; they were simpler: I wanted a blue corduroy jacket with the FFA emblem, a cross section of an ear of corn, on its back. It was a status symbol ranking close to a Tiger letter jacket, and I was not a prime candidate for a letter jacket.

The only one of the dozen creda of FFA that seemed to apply to my motives was "To provide and encourage the development of organized rural recreational activities."

I equated "rural recreational activities" with parking on secluded country lanes with my female classmates, none of whom as yet shared my enthusiasm. Thus I thought FFA would be a good way to meet girls, specifically the farmer's daughter of fable. I was wrong about that, too.

The Future Farmers of America is to agricultural aspirants as the army is to those who yearn for hand-to-hand combat. It is the organized, uniformed cadre of those who study agriculture in high school.

The organization began in Missouri in 1928. The first line of the FFA creed reads, "I believe in the future of farming, with a faith born not of words but of deeds . . ." This should have given me pause, had I bothered to consider its meaning.

For one thing, I was a town kid, even though my father owned a farm. Town kids in Keytesville High School FFA in the late 1940s were like women in the pool hall. It just wasn't done. There were farm boys and townies, and they did not intermingle.

But three of us townies decided to break tradition. Foster's father, like mine, was a rarity for the time, a man whose home was in town, but whose roots were on the farm. Foster's grandparents lived not too far north of Keytesville on a farm, and he regularly worked there.

Tommy Coy's father ran the "county farm," which is what we called the old folks' home. It really wasn't a farm; it was a place for indigent old people to go so they could die. But here was this tenuous link to the land: Foster's grandparents were farmers, my father owned a farm . . . and Tommy's father ran a geriatric "farm." Is it any wonder that we eagerly signed up for the Future Farmers of America?

Farming sounded romantic to us townies. What drawbacks could there be to the bucolic life? Outdoors all the time, soaking up sunshine and healthful vibrations. It would have saved much trouble had any of us asked a farm kid how much fun he had. He could have told us, for example, about slopping hogs in the dark of a bitter winter before sunrise, working in fields by tractor headlight after a long day at school, or bucking hay bales in the relentless Missouri summer heat.

We vaguely envisioned being one with the land, feeling the good earth squishing between our toes, and seeing crops blossom and fruit.

We needed a "project," a farm enterprise that authenticated our presence in FFA, so I acquired a Duroc gilt, a lovely red pig with long eyelashes and a virginal look that belied the fact that she was with child. God knows who the father was (I was supposed to, but my record keeping was not the stuff of which passing grades were made).

The romance of caring for this creature soon gave way to cold weather, sniffles, chapped hands, intestinal parasites (hers, not mine), manure, and the other realities of farming. I found that pigs, as self-reliant as they are, do require some supervision, winter and summer. The pig was mine in name only. I found a thousand reasons why I couldn't quite be there for her, and soon her care was given over to one of the tenant farmers. But even though I really didn't work on my project, I continued the fiction so I could stay in FFA and maybe find some raison d'être for me in agriculture.

Then, Foster found our Purpose: Each spring, Future Farmers across Missouri competed in agriculture-oriented events such as livestock judging. The district winners advanced to the state competition at Columbia.

The mere mention of Columbia set our juvenile juices a-stewing. Columbia was the Big Apple for Keytesville boys, most of whom had never been farther from home than Moberly. It was the Forbidden City. Chicago had long since faded from my memory, and anyway, I had lived there when I was pre-pubescent—I wouldn't have known a sin if I'd found one. But thanks to my Thorne Smith novels, I now knew all about sin in the abstract, but desperately wanted some hands-on experience.

Columbia is the home of the University of Missouri. Surely there was some hands-on experience waiting to be had in Columbia. If there was no sin in Columbia, with all those randy college students, then there was no sin in Missouri. We had to get there.

The first ever national vo-ag dairy judging had been won by a team from Keytesville in 1926, before there was a state FFA. They traveled all the way to Indianapolis, Indiana, which, for a Keytesville kid, was equivalent to being shot to Mars.

If a bunch of Chariton County rubes could win national honors, we intellectual townies ought to be able to breeze through regional competition and win a trip to Columbia. And there were theaters in Columbia that showed things you'd never see in a Doris Day movie: one showed foreign films, and we all knew what went on in foreign films.

We dreamed of roaming Columbia in the heat of the night, meeting experienced women who would lure us into sultry, dimly lit dens of pleasure, where we would experience the first sweet pangs of debauchery.

But first we had to qualify. We looked over the available competitions. We ruled out livestock judging in any form, because even the most casual farm boy knew more about the proper conformation of cows, pigs, and sheep than we ever would.

Besides, farm animals tended to be large and unpredictable. We'd all heard tales of sows getting farmers down in the pig yard and chewing off their legs. And a cow's eye was larger than most of my muscles. I wanted nothing to do with a creature that was far stronger than I and that perhaps had a dim perception that I was nurturing him to the slaughterhouse. Revenge is not necessarily beyond the ken of a male hog, especially after you've started his life by cutting off his nuts.

Live animals were out.

"Hey, look at this!" exclaimed Foster, our ringleader. "Seed judging!" It was buried in the fine print, a contest so minor that a real farm boy would have dismissed it in contempt. It was just what we were counting on: We needed a contest with no competition to maximize our chances for a trip to the big town.

We really didn't judge seeds; we identified them. It was a matter of memory, and there was no involvement with hoofed creatures.

Mr. Schmid, our vo-ag instructor, was baffled by town boys in agriculture. He was kind, but it was as if he had been asked to tutor Eskimos, whose way of life was totally foreign. He searched for common ground.

Once he took us on a field trip to castrate hogs and showed us how to do it with his teeth. The townies all got lightheaded, and Tommy trotted over behind a haystack and threw up. Mr. Schmid then asked for volunteers, and we three townies shrank to the back of the crowd. A farm boy eagerly knelt to the feast, his teeth snapping.

When we told Mr. Schmid we wanted to enter the FFA competition, he was delighted to see us finally interested in agriculture. "It'll help you all your lives to know one seed from another," he promised enthusiastically.

"Why can't we just look on the package if we want to know what's inside?" I asked. He looked at me for a long time, one of many such gazes to come.

But we decided to be the best damn seed-judging team KHS ever had (not to mention the first). We worked before and after school hours, pawing through seed samples and studying written material. At the district competition we blew out the opposition (one other team). We had our ticket to Columbia.

Columbia, if anything, proved duller than Keytesville. College students looked at us as if we'd just crawled out of a manure heap, and the foreign film we skulked in to see was incredibly boring. The only nude woman was built like Tugboat Annie and was dead.

Instead of finding a steamy boudoir, we fell into exhausted sleep on creaking army cots in company with five thousand other sweating Future Farmers in the university's Brewer Fieldhouse. The sultry air was filled with groans, moans, sneezes and snorts, coughing, and snoring, plus some other sounds.

Our choices were two: we could abandon FFA, or we could try again as sophomores to solve the riddle of Columbia (the riddle of agriculture was a lost cause). Surely, Columbia held more for us than the thousands of coughing, belching Blue-clads in Brewer Fieldhouse.

But first we needed another snap contest. Once you'd been in a competition, you could not repeat it. Foster studied the catalog.

"*Meat judging!*" Mr. Schmid exclaimed, aghast. We were joking with the gods of agriculture. We showed him the catalog. "Why don't you judge sheep or cows or something like everybody else?" he grumbled.

So we learned about marbling and other esoterica of the butcher, and we finished second (among three teams) in district competition. Good enough to send us on another expense-paid vacation to Brewer Fieldhouse. The same group of air swallowers had returned, noisier than ever, and the foreign film house was closed for lack of business.

Instead, we went to a mainstream movie house, which featured what must have been the last vaudeville act to play Missouri. A sweating fellow came out and announced that he would play two trombones at the same time.

"Yeah, but you got two heads!" shouted some balcony wit and we all roared. College humor was just as sophisticated as we'd imagined. Still, sitting in a movie house in Columbia watching terrible entertainment wasn't much different from being in Keytesville.

Then we became juniors. One last chance to pervert ourselves in the city. We studied the FFA competitions catalog far more assiduously than we ever did the *Soils Manual.*

No luck—we'd used up the easy competitions. It looked as if we might have to deal with live animals for the first time.

Foster's brow furrowed in concentration. This was a test of his skill at finding the easy way. Finally the worry lines smoothed, he turned to us with a broad smile.

"Chicken judging!" Mr. Schmid roared. "What's the matter with you boys, anyway?"

But judge chickens we did, and some basic misconceptions quickly cleared up. We had only a hazy notion of how you judge a chicken. First, we assumed it was chicken *meat* we would be asked to judge, like those steaks and chops from the year before. We assumed we would gaze upon the defunct bodies of chickens, rating their suitability for the roasting pan.

Our eyes glazed over when Mr. Schmid appeared with several live, smelly hens. They clucked, fussed and, worst of all, held their droppings in reserve until the moment when a fastidious chicken judger was most vulnerable.

For those who may not be familiar with the way laying chickens are judged, let me explain: Assume you are right-handed. You scoop up a chicken—not an easy task, since chickens resent such ignominy—and stuff her under your left armpit, tail to the front. Then, holding her immobile with your left arm, lift the tail with your left hand. The right hand contains the gauge by which you measure a chicken's egg-laying ability—your fingers.

If you remember the Boy Scout and Cub Scout salutes, you can judge chickens, because you give the hen a sort of Cub or Boy Scout salute, only horizontal, laying the two or three fingers against the egg vent to measure its span, which gives you an idea of how large an egg the chicken is capable of delivering.

If there is such a thing as a one-finger chicken, it is destined only for the pot. It would lay eggs an ambitious robin could beat. Two fingers (a Cub Scout chicken) probably is a pullet, an egg virgin. She may develop, but she is not yet a performer in the hot competitive atmosphere of big-time egg laying.

A three-finger chicken is the standard and goes to the henhouse to perform her matronly duties. She is a soldier in the trenches, reliable and productive.

Perhaps somewhere there is a four-finger chicken. He who owns a four-finger chicken is blessed. Egg producers dream of the four-finger chicken; a four-finger chicken could name its price in any henhouse in America.

That is what I learned in chicken judging. We went to the district meet, flexing our fingers, filled with competitive fire.

The top three teams would qualify for state. Since we had not yet been in a competition with more than three teams, we were confident. There were four teams and we finished fourth.

Mr. Schmid looked sadly at us and we hung our heads.

I decided that farming was not my vocation and told Mr. Schmid that I would not be taking vo-ag my senior year, nor would I be a member of FFA. His face cleared, the furrows smoothed from his brow, and he became expansive.

"My boy," he said, "what are your plans?"

"I dunno," I mumbled. "Maybe become a writer or something. . . ."

"Good! Good!" he exclaimed expansively. "Good!" He wandered off to a small group of freshmen who were wearing their new blue FFA jackets. Mr. Schmid had spent his life talking above the roar of tractors and was slightly deaf.

"That boy and his friends judged chickens," he bellowed in what he thought was a whisper. "Only chicken judges I ever had." Their eyes slewed toward me, as if they were looking at a two-headed calf.

I knew there would be no more chicken judges at Keytesville High School, that vo-ag at my high school had crossed a low-water bridge and would not return by the same route.

13

Pals

I must have been slightly ashamed of my father—at least defensive about what he did. I certainly didn't go around bragging that my dad had made his pile sniffing odiferous substances . . . and given our lifestyle, his pile was pretty modest.

I could point to a section of land in Kansas and even more acreage in north Missouri, but my friends saw me riding around in a decrepit Ford and living in a raggedy hotel with no running water, nor indoor facilities; all the big-time landowners they knew at least could go to the bathroom indoors and didn't have to scrounge drinking water from their tenants.

Every day at school, Foster's father was a constant presence, like a summer storm on the horizon. And the Sadlers had a television set and a new car.

Karl's father was a working farmer, and I knew from living with Sis and Finney what that life was like. But they had two vehicles and didn't bathe in a washtub.

My father left late and came home early. He puttered in his garden patches at the farm and, after the Hell Machine went back to its infernal stable, he did little physical work. Certainly, none of this—our current lifestyle, the fact that he'd sold perfume oils most of his adult life—was likely to create awe in Chariton Countians.

It took duck hunting to change my opinion of him . . . or more accurately, to allow me to form a positive one. My father and I started being friends when we started hunting ducks together.

Duck hunting, the way we did it, was shared misery, and there is nothing like nose-running cold to bring a couple of people together.

This maturation, if that's what it was, spanned four years, represented by four old hunting permits bought by my father, the first in 1947, the year we moved to Dalton.

They're among the effects left behind when he died. There really aren't many artifacts of my parents' life together—a couple of photo albums and a couple of boxes with miscellaneous papers in them. In one of those boxes I found the four old Missouri hunting permits, signed with his familiar elegant signature: Martin B. Vance.

My father bought a Missouri resident 1947 hunting permit that first year in Dalton. It cost $2.15. He bought it October 15, which is when the Missouri maples are on fire and the oaks are blushing.

There would be ducks in the Dalton bottoms, down by the Cutoff, and people were talking hunting in the B & J grocery store and at the post office and, especially, at the hardware store, where the owner, Tyson Knight, reigned, slouched back in an easy chair. People bought nails and lumber there, but they also bought shotgun shells.

Knight also owned the Dalton Cutoff Hunt Club, which was as good a duck hunting spot as existed in Missouri. In October and November it was a home for the incredible flight of mallards that shadowed the skies in the late 1940s and the early 1950s.

The Dalton Hardware Store was the gathering place for hunters headed to the Dalton Cutoff Hunt Club; Tyson Knight owned both businesses.

My father took me hunting with him at the Cutoff that first year, 1947. He dug deep into his shabby pocket and came up with enough money to rent a blind at the Cutoff—good blinds didn't come cheaply even then. This was before Karl and Foster and I had met the Hunt Club caretaker, so we put up with luck-of-the-draw for a blind.

I was dressed in a World War II navy surplus pea jacket, and I learned why a generation of swabbies despised those jackets: They aren't warm. They were designed by someone who never had to wear one in a Dalton Cutoff duck blind. The stiff fabric cut the harsh northwest wind some, but icy tendrils sneaked between the oversized buttons and down the loose neck.

I huddled into the thing, shivering, with my teeth chattering, and was miserable. I had been up since 4 A.M., and we were long hours from the occasionally warm furnace back at the hotel. My hands were numb, and I was discovering for the first time that blue jeans are not adequate winter clothing.

It's always colder in memory than it really was, but it's a rare year now when the Cutoff freezes solid. It did then with regularity.

The blind was on the east shore of what we called the "island," though it was merely a high spot in a large wooded marsh that extended to the west. Now, that marsh has been drained and the Cutoff is a big bathtub, surrounded by corn and bean fields. The big woods where the mallards splashed and gossiped is a ghost woods in my memory only.

That's all I remember about our first season on the Cutoff—that it was cold and I was cold. If we shot ducks I don't remember it, but we probably shot at more than we hit. My father had a Model 12 Winchester full choke, 32-inch barrel pump gun that he had gotten somewhere—maybe in exchange for a sawmill. It was and is among the finest-made guns ever, a marvel of engineering.

The full choke version was a duck hunter's gun, built to resist corrosion, rust, and invasive sand. There is no sound quite so evocative of a duck marsh as that of a Model 12 slide chuckling metallically as you chamber a round.

My father bought another permit in 1948. I didn't need one until I was sixteen, though I did need a federal waterfowl stamp—what everyone calls a "duck stamp." The permit price went to $4.15 in 1948, but the duck stamp still was $1.00. That year, I was fourteen and had a warmer coat. I don't remember what it was, but it wasn't that damn pea coat. I had had a year in the blind and knew what to expect, but I went anyway. The pull of the marsh and the excitement of ducks in the air was stronger than the prospect of being miserably cold. Such is the beginning of a hunter.

Harry Truman was a month away from what we were confident would be a humiliating defeat by Tom Dewey, but we didn't care. Couldn't stand the man. Accidental president. We didn't like Roosevelt, either. Missouri is a Democratic state, except where us Republicans held sway. We were embarrassed by Harry Truman, that crude haberdasher from Kansas City. What a contrast, to go from the elegant and eloquent Franklin Roosevelt to the plain-spoken Mr. Truman.

Inherited politics—Republican father.

We broke ice a quarter-inch thick all the way across the Cutoff to our blind on the east shore of the island. None of this sissy motor stuff—we rowed it, in an old wooden boat with about forty coats of paint on it. The ice chimed as it splintered and hen mallards gossiped loudly in the big flooded woods, and all the ducks there murmured in the pale darkness like a large crowd watching a distant event.

"Listen to that!" I exclaimed, and my father nodded, intent on his oars, breathing hard. He was, at that moment, not my father, but a fellow traveler on a magic journey. He was the only person I knew who could accompany me there. Karl and Foster, my best friends, could not—either because they couldn't afford it or because they didn't care enough.

But my father had arranged it, not for his hunting or fishing buddies, but for me. It was a moment of transition between a father and a son, and a father and a friend.

We broke the decoys free, rowing among them to shatter the thick ice film. They bobbed in the wash of the boat and tendrils of fog showed in the first light. Mallards whispered overhead, their wings creaking. I was back in the blind with an enormous 12-gauge double-barrel my father had got somewhere. He had his Model 12. The double has long since vanished, but the Model 12 survives, sleek and slick as then.

There were flights of mallards in the air everywhere. It was no trick to lure some into range—any hack caller could have brought them close in. A dozen made two passes overhead, their soughing passage like wind through pines.

"Take them!" my father exclaimed, and we stood—I was on the left and saw the birds just above the decoys, frantically scooping at the air beneath them, trying for altitude, and I shot at the flock, never mind picking out a target . . . and a bird faltered and dropped; the second barrel went off, pointed vaguely toward the birds, and I sat down hard, shaking.

The 1949 permit still was $4.15, but the duck stamp rose to $2.00. My father, the former city dude, was buying his permits earlier and earlier: his first was bought in October, the second in February, this one January 3.

I was a freshman in high school by then, a big timer, on the freshman basketball team. This was when we staked out our crude willow blind on the east shore of the Cutoff, down-lake and across from the island blind of the year before.

It was at the edge of Sasse's Hole, a "blue hole," where the Cutoff's muddy water somehow had undercut the sand dam between the two and flooded the hole with clear water. Maybe springs fed Sasse's Hole, but whatever the source, the hole was clear-blue and the Cutoff was muddy brown.

Across the lake from us, at the south tip of the island, was the large trucking company's blind, where the high rollers hunted. It was a fact that anyone in that blind was infinitely richer than we were and, considering the wealth of decoys sprayed in front of the blind, infinitely more likely to shoot at ducks. We got the spillover—ducks that circled wide enough to pass over us. Only rarely did they give our dozen decoys a look, and that probably was contemptuous. Ducks, being social creatures, much prefer the company of as many of their fellows as possible. Not a dozen, but many dozen.

The big blind on the island, with its cooking facilities, heat, comfortable seats (if it had them), was everything that ours wasn't. The northwest wind whistled across the Cutoff, rocking the huge decoy spread in front of the company blind, and our pitiful few blocks looked forlorn, lonely and, most of all, completely insufficient.

These were cold winters, too—global warming, if it exists, was not in evidence. Winter was winter and even when the Cutoff was free of ice, the wind that came down the lake, apparently direct from the polar ice cap, cut like a band saw.

There were Canada geese in Chariton County by then, beginning to congregate at Swan Lake National Wildlife Refuge, which was born in 1937. There were perhaps twenty thousand, a tenth of what comes there today. Sometimes they strayed into the Dalton bottom fields to feed. No bird is very bright, but Canada geese often make you wonder if you've unfairly underestimated avian intelligence.

We parked the car in the brittle silence of winter night, in the lea of a levee and across a wide field from our blind. We could see the ghostly pulse of our breath in the starshine and felt the quick bite of the air against exposed skin. The ground crackled as we stumbled across rough frozen clods.

Shortly after daylight, two Canada geese flew by over the Cutoff, set their wings, and glided into the stubble field behind us. "I'm going to sneak up on them," I told my father.

I didn't realize this was among history's greatest statements of misguided optimism. I slithered down a plow furrow as the rising sun devoured the frost and left a slime of gumbo atop the frozen ground. The stuff applied itself like paint.

I raised my head to peek after I figured I was within range. The geese seemed no closer than they had been. I ducked and crawled some more, raised my head. The geese were the same distance, still out of gun range. Even the most dense bumpkin has occasional flashes of understanding, so it finally occurred to me that the geese knew I was there, and that they were moving when I did, all the while keeping just out of shotgun range.

I got up, slathered with Chariton County gumbo, and the geese looked at me with mild interest, as if absently confirming what they already knew.

I slogged back through the mud and my father gave me a sympathetic smile. He didn't bother to state the obvious, that anyone with sense would not have wasted the time. Nor did he try to make me feel better by saying "Nice try" or something equally insufficient.

He just turned back to the lake, where a distant flight of mallards was circling. We heard calling from the blind across the lake and I silently mouthed words that my father would not have said out loud, but maybe he was saying them under his breath, too.

"I wish those guys would go home," I said. "They get everything."

He nodded and, I'm sure, was wishing he could do better by his kid, but he couldn't.

The ducks quit flying at midmorning, and the high rollers left the big blind; we saw them sling into their motorboats the ducks that they had shot, and then they jounced through the chop across to the Hunt Club for a hearty brunch and a few bumps of bourbon.

We waited a while, hoping that our turn had come, but nothing moved, and then we rose stiffly in the chill late November day and began the long walk back to the levee, where the old Ford was parked.

14

Winding Down

Hot day in late May 1952. The Chariton County air has a tinge of dust in it. Farmers working their fields, getting ready to plant corn and soybeans. Faint aroma of pig from the occasional hog farm.

Chariton County, land of row crops. The Chariton River cuts straight through the county, jerked straight by channelization. Already the old channel that winds through our farm near Bynumville is going stagnant.

Once in autumn I walked through the sun-dappled trees along the bank of the old channel, and two wood ducks had leaped into flight; I shot at them with the top-heavy double-barrel that my father had picked up somewhere. I missed.

The two ducks, refugees from a pop artist's palette, skittered through the shafts of sunlight, their colors almost lost among the fall reds and yellows, and I was glad that I had missed.

Already bulldozers are pushing the bank-side trees into the old channel, obliterating it to make way for bigger fields. This channelization is the end of the Chariton River as a rich ecosystem, and it's indicative of what is coming.

The big war has been over for nearly a decade, and the machines we developed to win it now are loose on the land as agricultural tools. Uncle Finney's team of horses is as anachronistic now as he is. The burning brushpile is a torch lighting the way to a megafarm future. My father is making plans to doze out the Bend, a chunk of bottom hardwoods where we hunted ducks when it was flooded, and where he hunted squirrels.

It can raise a few more bushels of soybeans, and more is better. Already my life is changing fundamentally, though I don't know it. My father never will realize that the simple pleasures, like squirrel hunting, are gone because he was seduced into believing he could do without a squirrel woods, but couldn't do without more cropland.

Graduation is now, not some distant date. It is tonight. And I will get a diploma, a ticket to the future. Forget the horror stories about dumb kids who got blank diplomas so they wouldn't be embarrassed on graduation night. I'll get one with my name on it, signed by school officials. I am the salutatorian of our class of twenty-three. Adeline Smith is the valedictorian. She paid attention, did her lessons promptly, and deserves the honor. I was looking at Miss Gerhardt's legs.

If starting high school was scary, my life ahead is even more so. Whatever insecurity I've felt for four years is nothing compared to the unknown void of college and beyond. I know everybody in Keytesville High School, but I will know no one at the University of Missouri; I will have to room with a stranger. For an unsure kid, the prospect is frightening.

We are gathered backstage in the gymnasium, talking nervously. Marleen is tiny and wonderfully cute in her gown. We gather in little knots of familiarity, huddling with those we've known for four years.

We will scatter like a covey of quail. Foster is headed for Central Methodist College where maybe he can play basketball. Gerald Linneman is going there, too, and will set a school in-

Senior class photo—with my hair greased and teased to perfection,
I am headed for the big university and the big unknown.

dividual game scoring record of fifty-three points. Gerald, the consummate athlete of Keytesville High School, will die before I do, and so will Foster.

A few are headed directly back to the tractor shed and will be there fifty years later. Marleen will be marrying her West Pointer. Karl is in the audience out front. He's only a junior.

I want to study journalism—it's all I've ever wanted—and the University of Missouri has one of the top two or three journalism schools in the country, so there's no choice as to where I am going. Going to Central Methodist just to be with buddies would be like going to South Dakota to study French culture. It can be done, but not very well.

No matter where I go to college, I will be on my own, as lonesome and disassociated from familiar things as I had been when we moved to Dalton. Even worse, I won't have a family close by, nor my disheveled rooms in the old hotel.

We'll have one last summer down home. Play some baseball, swim in Sasse's Hole, read some books, sit out on the ramshackle porch after dark, when the heat of the day has gone, and sing to the dark bulk of the Dalton elevator across the street.

Chairs clatter in the gym as people settle in for the graduation ceremony, coughing, rustling, whispering. A couple of little kids who could have been me the day I moved from Chicago wrestle in the vestibule. Farmers shift uncomfortably in their folding chairs, having spent the day riding uncomfortable tractor seats as they planted corn and beans.

The lights dim and everyone hushes as the school band raggedly plays the processional. It is our last big show, not a basketball game, not a junior or senior play, not even an assembly.

Dud Hayes, who had called balls and strikes (mostly balls when I was pitching) during most of the baseball games we'd played in high school, is president of the school board and hands out the diplomas with a handshake and a smile for each of us.

Perhaps somewhere Mr. Pegler and Miss Gerhardt are shuddering as if someone had walked over their graves. Perhaps somewhere they are teaching at the college level, living in terror that some shambling ignoramus from Keytesville High School will pop up in one of their classes, like a poisonous mushroom.

Or maybe I'm making too much of it. Maybe they realized that Karl and Foster and I were not among the failures, despite our smart-ass behavior. Or maybe they don't even remember us.

And then it is over. I move the mortarboard tassel from one side to the other, symbolic of graduation, and stumble off the stage into the darkened wings.

I know that once I break free of Chariton County, it never will be the same, that home will be a transitory way station. I can't imagine anything worse than taking over the farm and doing what my father does, which is stay out of the way.

I recognize—and I suspect he recognizes, too—that he is superfluous to the operation of the farm. It was done without him before we moved to Missouri, and it could be done without him again.

He is a man of such simple pleasures. He reads but has no other hobbies. I wish he were more forceful, recognizing that I'd be a better person if he had occasionally cracked a whip over me. And my mother is submissive to a passive man. They are so completely happy with each other. But I don't have an "each other." Just me.

There's too much restlessness in me, too much country unexplored beyond Moberly and even Columbia. I've heard the Morse code of ships at sea over our big radio, and I've read about the Left Bank of the Seine in our books.

My father reverted to his roots, became once again the kid in the shabby clothing with a fishing pole, and became for me a human being and a friend.

I want to write about life, something that I'd better start experiencing, because a fair chunk of it already is gone with nothing to show. Who would ever want to read about castrating hogs?

The hotel is doomed, though we don't know that. No matter that it is a historic landmark, built from the timbers of an even more historic icon, a Missouri River paddleboat. Sometime in the 1960s, after my parents move to a town fifty miles away, the new owners will tear the old hotel down. I hope the riverboat timbers, no doubt still as sinewy as they were driving the riverboat, are used in some stout new building—maybe a hog house.

I wonder if anyone will ever remember the weird kid who used to dribble a basketball back and forth along the shuddery veranda.

"Damndest thing I ever seen. Back and forth, back and forth. And every now and then the ball'd jump the railing and bounce across the street. Goofy-lookin' basketball, had a big pooch where the seam was ripped."

FFA, baseball, basketball . . . they all are past and so, as I hold my diploma, is high school.

A year later, though I don't know it, the girl I will marry will graduate from Macon High School and, near the end of my senior year in college, we'll meet on a blind date.

"You were," I will tell her forty years later, "the best kisser I ever met." Not, of course, explaining that the database was fairly limited.

Besides being a former prom queen, Marty has a unique throaty voice and is slender and petite. And she has those lush lips. I will think she is the most graceful human I've known and wonder why she agrees to go out with me more than once. It's not unreasonable to wonder whether she thinks the same.

Foster and I will spend the next thirty years hanging around with each other. He will get me interested in skiing, bicycling, caving, canoeing, backpacking, and a host of other outdoor activities. We'll make trips together to the Black Hills and Wisconsin's Bois Brule River, to Arkansas and South Dakota and Iowa.

We'll canoe hundreds of miles together, alone and with our families. Our kids will grow up together. We'll spend countless

Today there is nothing left of the old hotel but some cracked
concrete and junk tires, thrown on the seedbed of my life.

hours quail hunting in the hills and bottoms of the Mussel Fork, sleeping in the old farmhouse that belonged to Foster's grandparents.

We'll turkey hunt on the ridges of their farm, amid Indian mounds where, if you are of an active imagination, you can feel a ghostly presence in the chill mist of dawn.

Foster's dark turns of mind come when he isn't with me. Maybe I am his release or relief or escape. I don't ask, and he doesn't volunteer. But there is a depression in him that is stronger than his will to repel it.

And then, one cold, snowy January day, he will blow away his demons, and I will miss him for the rest of my life.

Karl and I will room together his freshman year at the university, but it is a bad idea. A couple of his football jock friends with a couple of other football jocks will decide to make our room their headquarters. They, along with their enormous teammates, will play endless games of Monopoly, mostly on my bed, and I will spend hours in the dorm lounge trying to study, falling asleep, waiting for those Neanderthal linemen to go home. Karl and I will remain friends, but decide that rooming together was a mistake.

He'll go into Naval ROTC, take a Marine Corps commission, get his leg shot up in Vietnam, and retire as a colonel. Now he's recovering from a stroke, but he is still not fully mobile. He'd have a tough time playing burnout.

Country Club and Griesidieck beer have vanished long ago. I don't know about English Ovals—I will quit smoking when my father dies of smoking-related causes.

I once went back to Sis and Finney's farm, the place where I spent my first summers down home. Sis, Finney, and my

The farmstead down home is empty of those who once lived there—they rest a half mile up the road in Asbury Cemetery. I look at the old place where I spent so many days as a kid and wonder where the years went.

grandfather, now lie in the Asbury Cemetery, a half-mile up the road. The big maples in the front yard still were there, bent a bit more, but aren't we all? The house was empty, echoing with ghosts of Grandpa Vance and Uncle Finney and Aunt Sis. Yet no smell of drop biscuits, nor woodsmoke from the Warm Morning kitchen stove, no yellow, warm light from a coal-oil lamp—just a damp mustiness that stuck in my nose.

The tobacco barn was swaybacked and sagging, doors canted on rusted hinges. Pigweed grew where the pigs used to be, beneficiary of their countless deposits.

Virginia Woolf said, "Barns and summer days in the country, rooms where we sat all now lie in the unreal world which is gone."

I prowled around the little house, which had seemed so

Beyond salvage now, Finney's tobacco barn is a shambles. Only memories remain of sitting in the haymow door with the girl down the road and waiting for life to begin.

much larger when I was so much smaller. The boards creaked under my feet and the wallpaper was loose and ragged.

I went outside and looked at the old barn on a gray winter day and tried to recall the warmth of summer, the sound of cicadas, and the silvery laugh of the girl down the road, but I couldn't do it.

I shivered and turned away as the cold wind pushed the dangling loft door and made the remaining hinge moan. I heard voices in that rusty cry that caused a sudden chill.